Suzan-Lori Parks

Deborah R. Geis

THE UNIVERSITY OF MICHIGAN PRESS

ANN ARBOR

Published in the United States of America by
The University of Michigan Press
Manufactured in the United States of America
⊗ Printed on acid-free paper

2011   2010   2009   2008   4   3   2   1

A CIP catalog record for this book is available from the British Library.

Library of Congress Cataloging-in-Publication Data

Geis, Deborah R., 1960–
    Suzan-Lori Parks / Deborah R. Geis.
       p.   cm. — (Michigan modern dramatists)
    ISBN-13: 978-0-472-09946-7 (cloth : alk. paper)
    ISBN-10: 0-472-09946-9 (cloth : alk. paper)
    ISBN-13: 978-0-472-06946-0 (pbk. : alk. paper)
    ISBN-10: 0-472-06946-2 (pbk. : alk. paper)
       1. Parks, Suzan-Lori—Criticism and interpretation.   I. Title.

    PS3566.A736Z69   2008
    812'.54—dc22   2008011492

Suzan-Lori Parks

MICHIGAN MODERN DRAMATISTS
Enoch Brater, Series Editor

Michigan Modern Dramatists offers the theatergoer concise, accessible, and indispensable guides to the works of individual playwrights, as interpreted by today's leading drama critics. Forthcoming books in the series will consider the works of Sam Shepard, Samuel Beckett, and Wendy Wasserstein.

TITLES IN THE SERIES
Edward Albee by Toby Zinman
Suzan-Lori Parks by Deborah R. Geis

Acknowledgments

So many people have responded to my efforts in writing this book with unflagging wisdom, wit, support, and generosity of spirit; I am deeply indebted to all of them. At the University of Michigan Press, my heartfelt thanks to LeAnn Fields for her interest in and tireless help with the project, to her assistants Anna Szymanski and Catherine Cassel, and to Marcia LaBrenz and Richard Isomaki. As always, I am grateful to Enoch Brater for his shining example and ongoing mentorship. I thank the two anonymous readers who commented on the manuscript of the project and made highly helpful suggestions. This project would not have been the same without the kindness of Suzan-Lori Parks, who not only wrote such dazzling plays, but who also responded graciously to my barrage of questions.

For sharing information about their wonderful productions and for their generosity in permitting me to use the photographs they provided, I am deeply grateful to the following people: Jason Bruffy and the Know Theatre of Cincinnati, Gigi Fenlon and DePauw University Theatre, Rob Melrose and the Cutting Ball Theater Company of San Francisco, Kyle Shepherd and the Actors Theatre of Louisville, Allison Eve Zell and HERE/The Mint Space, New York City.

Portions of this book were presented in earlier form at several conferences, including those of the American Literature Association, the Modern Language Association, the Literature- Film Association, and the Twentieth Century Literature Conference. My thanks to the conference and panel organizers for enabling me to share my work in progress, and to the attendees of these sessions for their provocative questions. The discussion of Parks's "red letter" plays was published in earlier form in the *Journal of American Drama and Theatre* 16.2 (Spring 2004), and I thank the editors of this publication for their permission to reprint.

At DePauw University, our staff members—especially Department of English secretary Bobbi Kelley, and Terry Bruner in Faculty

Development—have assisted me virtually every single day, and I deeply appreciate their work. Thanks to Neal Abraham, Meryl Altman, Robert Bottoms, Tom Chiarella, Vanessa Dickerson, Gigi Fenlon, Wayne Glausser, Eugene Gloria, Peter Graham, Joe Heithaus, Ronda Henry, James Lincoln, William G. Little, Marnie McInnes, Keith Nightenhelser, Greg Schwipps, Mike Sinowitz, Andrea Sununu, Chris White, and Lili Wright for the extra steps they took to support this project and to facilitate Ms. Parks's visit to our campus.

Many thanks, as always, to my mother, Dorothy Geis, and to my sisters, Nancy Geis Bardgett and Sarah Geis, for their warmth and support. More than they realize, the following people have meant the world to me in their ongoing friendship and guidance: Maura Abrahamson, Joyce Ann, Anthony Barone, Tracy and Reinold Cornelius, Steven F. Kruger, Ed Ku, Kathleen Moore, Janet Pennisi, Claudia Petersen, Ron Scapp, Peter Schamel, Meryl Siegman, Robert Vorlicky, Karen Vrotsos, David J. Weiss, and Regina Wilmes. And nothing would be possible without the ability of James S. Bennett and his son, Alexander Bennett, to share my life and make me laugh.

Contents

Introduction:
Under the Piano and All That Jazz
Biography, Influences, Themes, Style

> I hear the sound of digging. A sound I know pretty well cause I done heard it so many times. You hear a lot of digging sounds in my line of work.
>
> —*Getting Mother's Body*

> HEAD DIGGER. Here is the well. Dig here.
> (*The Diggers dig. As they dig, they sing.*)
>
> —*Where is the Well?* (*365 Days/365 Plays* 59)

Contemporary playwright Suzan-Lori Parks is the most recognized and innovative dramatist of her generation. Winner of the 2002 Pulitzer Prize in Drama for her play *Topdog/Underdog* (and the first African-American woman playwright to win this award), Parks has created a significant body of work—including screenplays and a novel as well as a very substantial number of plays—and her drama is now part of the American theatrical canon. Her works have been produced around the country and internationally; she has been a MacArthur Fellow; and she has most recently served as the director of the playwriting program at the California Institute for the Arts.

Parks's works confront cultural constructions of history and literature. *Venus*, her play about Saartjie Baartman, who was exhibited as the "Venus Hottentot" in the nineteenth century, has been of interest to anthropologists and scientists who study the ongoing fascination with Baartman. At the turn of the millennium, Parks's paired "red letter" plays, *In the Blood* and *Fucking A,* rewrote Hawthorne's *The Scarlet Letter* with a new look at the classic character of Hester.

Parks's style is unlike that of any other playwright: she draws upon the jazz aesthetic of "repetition and revision"; she has invented a technique called the "spell"; and each of her works presents a new challenge to the audience—for example, parts of *Fucking A* are in an invented language. She also revises conventional notions about the construction of character: in *Last Black Man,* for instance, the characters (if one may call them that) include figures with names like "Lots of Grease and Lots of Pork" and "Yes and Greens Black-Eyed Peas Cornbread." As these qualities may suggest, Parks's plays are widely produced but are also extremely challenging. This volume— for general readers and spectators, teachers and directors, and students—offers an understanding of Parks's aesthetic that both analyzes her individual works and locates them in larger contexts. At present, Parks's works are studied in courses on American and African-American literature, on drama, and on postmodernism; outside of the academy, her works are staged in theaters around the world, and she is the subject of ongoing media attention (recently, for example, as a screenwriter for the film adaptation of Zora Neale Hurston's *Their Eyes Were Watching God*). The chapters that follow examine her works in detail, from the earliest experimental pieces like *Pickling,* to the hugely popular *Topdog/Underdog,* to her wide-ranging forays into fiction, music, and film.

To begin, it is worth taking a panoramic look at Parks's background, literary and theatrical influences, themes, and unique style.

From the Fort to the Lighthouse: A Biographical Sketch

Parks's background—followed by her literary and dramatic influences—provides a helpful starting point for understanding her work. While her plays are far less overtly autobiographical than those of, say, Ntozake Shange or Adrienne Kennedy, we can see her own past in her drama.

Suzan-Lori Parks was born on May 10, 1964 (she points out that she shares a birthday with John Wilkes Booth [Sova 32]) in Fort Knox, Kentucky, the second of three children (she has an older sister, Stephanie, and a younger brother, Donald ["Buddy"]). Her father, also named Donald, was an army colonel (a family setup that figures prominently in *Imperceptible Mutabilities in the Third Kingdom*), and her mother, Francis, was a teacher who provided strong encouragement for her children to read and write. As a child, Parks says, she made up a song about everything (Parks, "An Evening"). At the age of five, she started writing novels (Garrett 22), which she would compose as she sat underneath the family's baby grand piano. In fourth grade, she created with her brother a family newspaper called *The Daily Daily* and says, "We'd type it every day in our attic" (Miller and Cotliar 2).

As the result of her father's military career, Parks lived in many places as a child, including North Carolina, California, Kentucky, Texas, Vermont, Maryland, and Germany, where she was enrolled in a junior high school, "not speaking a word of the language" but learning it as she spent four years there (Solomon 79). TALK, her invented language in *Fucking A*, shows strong German influences, and the style of her plays as a whole forces readers and actors to learn a new tongue, as it were (see the discussion of language later in this chapter). Parks has said, "I've heard horrible stories about 12-step groups for army people. But I had a great childhood. My parents were really into experiencing the places we lived" ("Suzan-Lori Parks" 1). But she also felt profoundly the effect of her father's being gone for long periods of time, echoed in both *Imperceptible Mutabilities* and *The Death of the Last Black Man in the Whole Entire World*; Alice Rayner and Harry J. Elam comment that "[f]rom her perspective, her father 'died' in these periods only to be reborn upon return. When he did return, her mother would immediately attempt to feed him" ("Unfinished Business" 458). Parks told interviewer Shelby Jiggetts, "At one time we were moving every year. I think moving around had an influence on my writing" (310).

Back in the States for the last few years of high school, Parks was, because of her allegedly poor spelling, discouraged from writing by an English teacher, who told her that she should become a scientist. Parks entered Mount Holyoke College in South Hadley, Massachusetts, as a chemistry major. Parks eventually affirmed her love of literature after reading Virginia Woolf: *To the Lighthouse,* she says, "pulled me from the science lab into the literature lab" (Jiggetts 310). She changed her majors to English and German, graduating cum laude and Phi Beta Kappa in 1985. A turning point came when she took a fiction-writing seminar with the great author James Baldwin at Hampshire College. Baldwin encouraged her to turn to playwriting; his support was "like a kiss on the forehead to ward off all evil" (Miller and Cotliar 2). She adds, "I had a lot of heart, and I loved writing. And I think that's what he saw. He believed in me when I couldn't" (Bryant 43). Parks's first "real" piece of writing, a short story called "The Wedding Pig," was "about a school teacher in a small Texas town who attends a violent harvest ritual that goes dramatically awry." While writing the story she felt a "wave of psychic energy" going through her body, and knew that she would become a writer: "The story had elements of sex, love, violence, history and ritual, all connected—and all five of those elements have been around a long time in my work" (Sova 32). Her senior project at Mount Holyoke was her first play, *The Sinner's Place,* which won her honors in English but which the theater department refused to produce: "You can't have dirt on stage. That's not a play," she was told. However, Mary McHenry, an English department professor, gave her a copy of Adrienne Kennedy's *Funnyhouse of a Negro* and "made me understand that I can do anything I want" (Garrett 24; Jiggetts 310).

After graduation Parks spent a year in London, studying acting at the Drama Studio, and then moved to New York City, where she took a secretarial course and "learned how to type very quickly" (Parks, "An Evening"). She worked as a legal assistant and at various other jobs while she attempted to start her career as a playwright, beginning in 1987 with productions like *Betting on the Dust Commander* at a bar called the Gas Station (see discussion in the next chapter). By 1989, when Parks was barely twenty-five and had received important critical notice for *Imperceptible Mutabilities*, the *New York Times* named her "the year's most promising new playwright." Her career thereafter will be discussed throughout this study: Obie-winning off-Broadway plays, a five-hundred-thousand-dollar MacArthur "genius" grant in 2001 (among myriad other grants), and a production on Broadway of the Pulitzer Prize–winning *Topdog/Underdog*. Along this route, she penned the screenplay for Spike Lee's film *Girl 6* in 1996 (see the last chapter for a fuller discussion of her film work). In 1998, she met blues musician Paul Oscher, a former harmonica player for Muddy Waters, and married him in July 2001; while the blues is one of several musical influences that resonate throughout Parks's work, it is particularly evident in the novel she wrote during this period, *Getting Mother's Body* (see the last chapter in this book). As a mentor to developing playwrights, she taught at Yale and the New School, and took a position as director of the ASK Theatre Projects Writing for Performance Program at the California Institute for the Arts.

Mothers (and Fathers) of Invention: Influences

> Read me by repetition. Saints and singing and a mission and
> an addition.
> Saints and singing and the petition. The petition for a repetition.
> Saints and singing and their singing.
> Saints and singing and winning and
> Do not repeat yourself.
>> —Gertrude Stein, *Saints and Singing*
>> (*A Stein Reader* 399)

> I find there are no places only my funnyhouse.
>> —Adrienne Kennedy, *Funnyhouse of a Negro*
>> (*Adrienne Kennedy in One Act* 7)

Parks mentions frequently that her first major influence was the writer James Baldwin, with whom she took a fiction-writing course in college. When it was time to workshop her pieces in class, she would stand up and perform all of the characters (Bryant 43). Baldwin asked her whether she had considered playwriting. Parks listened, she has said, because "[s]omeone I respected was telling me what to do—in a good way. It wasn't some Whosey-Whatsit who runs La Fuddy Duddy Playhouse in Whosey-Whatsitville" (Garrett 22). As the renowned author of such works as *Go Tell It on the Mountain* and *Another Country*, Baldwin was influential in claiming an identity as a black writer in an era when doing so was a politically charged act, and in insisting that the African-American past be reclaimed into history. In "Many Thousands Gone," an essay in *Notes of a Native Son*, Baldwin writes words that Parks seems to have incorporated into her thinking about history and ancestry and about the speaking body: "In the case of the Negro the past was taken from him whether he would or no; yet to forswear it was meaningless and availed him nothing, since his shameful ['heathen'] history was carried, quite literally, on his brow" (29).

In her own reading and as a college student Parks was introduced to the pivotal modernist writers, including James Joyce, Gertrude Stein, Samuel Beckett, William Faulkner, and Virginia Woolf. Reading Woolf's *To the Lighthouse* restored her at a time when Parks felt discouraged about the possibility of majoring in English: "I remembered who I was," she remarks; "Virginia Woolf's novel re-membered me—it put me back together because it reminded me of what I loved" (Parks, "An Evening"). Parks has said that Faulkner is her favorite of the modernists and that she is "fascinated with what they were allowed to do . . . What Joyce was allowed to do or what Joyce allowed himself to do, what Beckett allowed himself to do, what Faulkner allowed himself to do, Woolf . . . What they got away with" (Drukman 72). Stein's influence can be seen throughout Parks's work, from the use of repetition (as in Stein's *A Circular Play / A Play in Circles*, or in *Saints and Singing*) to the experimentation with language (see, for example, Stein's *Reread Another / A Play / To Be Played Indoors or Out / I Want to Be a School*). Those who respond to Parks's work sometimes express surprise that these now canonical white writers exerted such a profound influence on her artistic aspirations. But their use of stream-of-consciousness, their willingness to break from conventions of sentence structure and language, and their assertion of voices that countered received wisdom were powerful examples to Parks.

African-American writers who influenced Parks included not only Baldwin but also Zora Neale Hurston, whose 1937 novel *Their Eyes Were Watching God* she would adapt in a screenplay decades after first reading it. Hurston, who traveled through much of her career as an anthropologist studying black folklore and dialects, fed Parks's interest in creating a stage language that pays close attention to sounds and that reflects the punning, inversions, creative substitutions, and metaphor that can be witnessed in Hurston's work. Hurston preserved and recorded ways of speaking and telling tales as a historical mission, at the same time using this material for her own fiction and drama. While Parks is more obviously a stylist in appropriating vernacular language and storytelling (including minstrelsy), she is playing off the legacy of Hurston in creating new histories (or new ways of telling history) that implicitly or explicitly critique the dominant ways of telling.

Parks also paid attention to two black women playwrights whose careers began in the mid-1960s and mid-1970s, respectively: Adrienne Kennedy and Ntozake Shange. Kennedy first received critical attention when her play *Funnyhouse of a Negro* was produced by Barr, Albee, and Wilder, who also produced LeRoi Jones's *Dutchman*, in 1964 (the year that Parks was born). Shange was the first African-American woman since Lorraine Hansberry to have a play on Broadway, with the 1975–76 *for colored girls who have considered suicide/when the rainbow is enuf*. A brief look at both playwrights' styles and themes reveals Parks as their figurative daughter and sister.

Adrienne Kennedy, who has said that her most powerful influences were Federico García Lorca and Tennessee Williams (Parks also acknowledges Williams's influence [Jiggetts 309]), creates a surrealistic form of poetic drama. "My plays are meant to be states of mind," she has remarked (*People* 127). Rosette Lamont, in her introduction to one of the first anthologies to feature Parks's work, notes that Kennedy (like Marita Bonner before her) "turned away from realism and used the avant-garde idiom" (xxxi).In her autobiographical collage *People Who Led to My Plays,* Kennedy says that she also draws upon elements as diverse as the movie star magazines she loved as a child ("I kept stacks of *Modern Screen* in the vanity table drawer" [33]) and the African political events of her young adulthood, such as the 1961 murder of a black hero, Congo prime minister Patrice Lumumba ("I felt I had been struck a blow" [119]). Plays like *Funnyhouse of a Negro, The Owl Answers,* and *A Movie Star Has to Star in Black and White* eschew conventional plot and character in favor of repetition (which Parks transmutes into "rep and rev"), fractured characters who sometimes speak chorally or share lines (such as Sarah the Negro in *Funnyhouse,* who speaks with Jesus, Patrice Lumumba, and others, or Clara in *Movie Star,* who lets Bette Davis and others say her lines for her), and surreal images (like the madwoman holding her own head in her hands in *Funnyhouse*). As Robert Vorlicky points out in his perceptive essay about the influence of Kennedy on playwright Tony Kushner, Parks draws upon not only Kennedy's surrealism, but also her predilection for monologues (5–6). Kennedy, like Parks, is interested in African-American history on both autobiographical and archetypal levels, but resists the direct political voice of Black Arts playwrights (LeRoi Jones / Amiri Baraka, Ed Bullins) in favor of a more visual and poetic, more personal (and, one might argue, more feminist) approach to seeing history anew. Parks did not meet Kennedy until 1993, when they, along with Ntozake Shange, were on a panel about African-American women playwrights; Parks and Kennedy hit it off immediately, and Parks persuaded Kennedy to join her in a visit to Disneyland (Ben-Zvi 206–7). Parks comments, "I like Adrienne Kennedy because she made me feel like I could do anything at that moment" (Jiggetts 314); Kennedy's work "inspired [her] to take weird riffs and shifts of character" (Solomon 75).

Ntozake Shange, who drew upon her dance training to perform her "choreopoems" at coffeehouses in the Bay Area, made a huge impact in 1975 when *for colored girls who have considered suicide/when the rainbow is enuf* was performed at a bar called DeMonte's on New York City's Lower East Side, then at the Henry

Street Settlement, then off-Broadway at the Public Theater, and then on Broadway in September 1976 (*See No Evil* 16). Media coverage of the play tended to focus on the closing "beau willie brown" sequence as an example of male-bashing. Far more important, though—and what Shange carried into her later works, such as *Spell #7*—was the unique fashioning of the play text, spinning and dancing free from Western conventions of language and presentation. In a program note, she writes:

> i cant count the number of times I have viscerally wanted to attack deform n maim the language that i was taught to hate myself in . . . the straitjacket that the english language slips over the minds of all americans. there are thoughts that black people just dont have/ according to popular mythology/so white people never "imagine" we are having them/& black people "block" vocabularies we perceive to be white folks' ideas. this will never do. (*See No Evil* 21)

Shange's texts are written in poetic form, with few stage directions, and with a close attention to speech as containing sound and move-ment. Her "colored girls'" journeys to self-discovery are closely bound to their ability to claim images and language, with the free-dom to narrate and create their agency, both collective (as women of color) and individual. Ben-Zvi suggests that, whereas Shange creates a self that emerges through her own language, Parks is interested in the political effects of competing ways of using language (cf. *Venus*): she "offers less a face beneath a mask—a language beneath a lan-guage—than the play between discourses" (191). Nevertheless, the legacy of Shange's dramatic voicings is evident. While Kennedy's work inspired Parks's fragmentation of characters and diminishment of plot in favor of repeated and unfolding stories, Shange influenced her freedom with language, specifically the freedom to rebel against white, Western standardizations of English. In both playwrights, lan-guage is deeply connected to the speaking characters bodied forth on stage; the unconventional look of the text reflects the need to find an Africanist-feminist way of speaking (for further discussion, see Geis, *Postmodern Theatric(k)s*, chap. 6).

Can You Dig It? Some Recurring Themes

African-American dramatists are often expected to reflect "the black experience" in everything they write, without accounting for multiplicities, differences across class and gender, and varying political and artistic outlooks. Parks is intent on avoiding this "essentialist" attitude: "[T]here is no single 'Black Aesthetic' and there is no one way to write or think or feel or dream or interpret or be interpreted" ("Equation" 21); her "New Black Math" expands creatively upon this idea (see the discussion in the last chapter of this book). Her resistance to being pigeonholed is reflected, in part, in the wide number of styles and genres with which she has experimented, as well as her insistence that the (white) modernists were as important an influence upon her writing as authors like Baldwin, Hurston, Kennedy, and Shange. At the same time, it is possible to define themes and stylistic choices that run through her work, and to characterize not only her political and historical outlook, but also her aesthetic choices for conveying it.

Kimberly W. Benston has argued that "[a]ll Afro-American literature may be seen as one vast genealogical poem that attempts to restore continuity to the ruptures or discontinuities imposed by the history of the black presence in America" (qtd. in H. Gates 123). While Parks may not see such "genealogical revisionism" as her project, discontinuous and violated genealogies, legacies, and ancestry are paramount in her work. *The Death of the Last Black Man in the Whole Entire World* warns repeatedly of the consequences of history that has been forgotten or rewritten by oppressors: the Yes and Greens Black-Eyed Peas Cornbread figure says, "You should write it down because if you dont write it down then they will come along and tell the future that we did not exist" (104). Yet the recording of history, Parks suggests, is not itself an act to be trusted. "I can get more out of history if I joke with it than if I shake my finger and stomp my feet," she says (Pearce 26). As Shawn-Marie Garrett points out, "Parks shows that history is and always has been as much enemy as ally to the collective memories and shared secrets of a black people jettisoned into a white world" (26). In her essay "Possession," Parks writes:

> Since history is a recorded or remembered event, theatre, for me, is the perfect place to "make" history—that is, because so much African-American history has been unrecorded, dismembered, washed out, one of my tasks as playwright is to—through literature and the special strange relationship between theatre and real-life—locate the ancestral burial ground, dig for bones, find bones, hear the bones sing, write it down. (4)

In all of her works Parks plays on the trope of remembering/dismembering, with all of its punning meanings. The act of memory is key, and the *re-* is a reminder that it must occur repeatedly, which ties into the "rep and rev" of her texts. To dis member in this sense is to forget. The sense of *member* as limb (or sometimes the penis) is also crucial, invoking the long history of lynching and other forms of torture: characters in her plays, such as the Venus Hottentot, are literally taken apart and put back together again through the act of memory (the remains of Saartjie Baartman, the real Venus, were dissected and pickled by Georges Cuvier; the play is a means of putting her back together again, even while it shows the impossibility of doing so). To be a member is also to belong to something; since African-Americans have been deprived of full membership as citizens, Parks is also re-membering them in the sense of putting them back onto the roster, back into the historical narratives from which they have been displaced, and rewriting (re-membering) those historical narratives in the process.

A related theme resonating through Parks's works is that of digging. "You find your voice by digging," she says. "Lots of my characters dig" (Fraden 40). To dig is both to excavate something that has been buried (like the forgotten parts of African-American history), and, in now-dated Beat vernacular, to understand. Some of Parks's plays have literal diggers: Brazil in *The America Play*, for instance, is digging up his father's past, and the Negro Resurrectionist in *Venus* earned his name because he once dug up cadavers for medical schools, but he now is emceeing the digging up / re-membering of the Venus Hottentot. Parks has said that the abrasive rhyme of *digger*/"*nigger*" is intentional. Digging also works symbolically in many of her pieces; the entire text of *The Death of the Last Black Man in the Whole Entire World* involves the unburying or unearthing of the African-American past in order to put the Black Man, whose death is restaged throughout the production, to rest.

Linked to both re-membering and digging is the trope of resurrection. The Black Man with Watermelon dies and comes back repeatedly in *Last Black Man*; the Foundling Father in *The America Play* and Lincoln in *Topdog/Underdog* are "assassinated" by tourists over and over; the Venus Hottentot dies and is brought back to life in the "countdown" narrative; and so on. As Harry Elam and Alice Rayner point out, "The notion of resurrection is consistent with much of Parks's work that points to how theatrical performance revivifies history, and how history is already performative" ("Body Parts" 275). One digs in order to resurrect; one resurrects in order to re-member. It is possible that Parks is influenced by her childhood Catholicism (and as the chapter "Choral Explorations of Race and Politics" discusses, so is the structure of *Last Black Man*), but her interest in resurrection—which includes bringing back literary and historical characters, like the re-envisioned Hesters in the red-letter plays—is inherently a *theatrical* way of imagining history. In the theater, characters start their stories all over again every night, and twice on matinee days. The power to resurrect is the power to repeat history. While scripted dramatic characters are compelled to reiterate the plot intended for them (hence Rosencrantz and Guildenstern's angst in Tom Stoppard's play about fate and *Hamlet*), Parks is fascinated by the tension between this limbo of repetition and the small variations within (it is a truism that no two performances of a play are exactly the same). As shall be discussed shortly, this fascination manifests itself through her use of repetition and revision. But it also links thematically to her renarrating history so that the lost past (again, particularly the African-American past) is resurrected and retold.

Signifyin, Spells, and Style

Parks uses an idiosyncratic, poetic form of theater language that is truly her own and that creates a deliberate form of resistance to "norms" of theatrical discourse. "I write to be read aloud," she says (Drukman 69), and adds, "Language is a physical act. It's something which involves your entire body—not just your head" ("Elements of Style" 11). When the text is performed, the audience, following the flow of the dialogue and the slangy, stichomythic exchanges, may not be aware of the care with which Parks has created a resistant, complicated textual statement. From her earliest work she omits punctuation, spells words ("thuh") according to their pronunciation, uses footnote numbers, and so on. "Look at the difference between 'the' and 'thuh,'" she writes in "Elements of Style." "The 'uh' requires the actor to employ a different physical, emotional, vocal attack" (12). The same essay includes a glossary of what she calls "foreign words and phrases," explaining the sound and meaning of locutions she is fond of, such as "ssnuch," "chuh," and "gaw" (17). Her comment about the significance of writing "k" instead of "o.k." is illuminating:

> It's a recording of, not only the way words sound, but what that means. The difference between "k" and "o.k." is not just what one might call black English versus standard English, for example. Or black English versus mid-Atlantic English. It's not that, so much as it's an attempt: I am trying to be very specific in what's going on emotionally with the character. Because if you just try out, "I'm going with you, O.K.," "I'm going with you, K," it's a different thing going on. If you jump to that word faster, if you put your words together in a different order, you're feeling something differently, and it's just an attempt to try to be more specific. (Jiggetts 311)

It would be oversimplifying to say that Parks writes in African-American vernacular, though that is certainly a component of her linguistic style. Kimberly Dixon explains that it is "grounded in African-American vernacular but extends beyond political definitions of articulateness to examine speech as a political process" (52).

I would add that Parks is also making an aesthetic and visual-aural choice as an artist; like a painter or musician, her choices riff on those of some of her predecessors, but also help embody what *distinguishes* her work as an individual creator.

Oral traditions associated with African-American culture—work songs, blues, jazz, call-and-response, sermons, and minstrelsy and vaudeville—show up in various ways in Parks's work, making a striking combination with her more "literary" use of modernist wordplay and stream-of-consciousness and her postmodernist use of intertexts, footnotes, media, and other referential devices. Yet the combination is not jarring if we realize that her collagelike style is not only a contemporary artist's freedom to draw upon any and all sources, but owes a great deal to the African-based tradition of "signifyin" and to the jazz-inspired "rep and rev" discussed subsequently. Parks tells Alisa Solomon:

> At one time in this country, the teaching of reading and writing to African-Americans was a criminal offense. So how do I adequately represent not merely the speech patterns of a people oppressed by language (which is the simple question) but the patterns of a people whose language use is so complex and varied and ephemeral that its daily use not only Signifies on the non-vernacular language forms, but on the construct of writing as well. If language is a construct and writing is a construct and Signifyin(g) on the double construct is the daily use, then I have chosen to Signify on the Signifying. (Solomon 76)

If postmodern African-American culture is a repository of these traditions, intentionally bent, twisted, and appropriated as both homage and critique, then Parks's combining them is also a way of creating an artistic voice that is uniquely hers yet speaks profoundly about the past and present.

Central to Parks's aesthetic is the idea of "rep and rev," or "repetition and revision." She comments, "I'm working to create a dramatic text that departs from the traditional linear narrative style to look and sound more like a musical score" ("Elements of Style" 9). We can see its antecedents both in jazz music and in the tradition of "signifyin." Jazz relies on the introduction of a main melodic theme followed by variations that improvise upon this theme but do not repeat it exactly. Steven Drukman remarks, "The 'rep and rev' strategy keeps the spectator/reader ever vigilant, looking for something missed in the last repetition while scrutinizing the upcoming revision. Closure seems just on the horizon . . . where it remains" (57). Parks adds that the "rev" is what keeps the "rep" interesting: "[I]n drama change, revision, is the thing. Characters refigure their words and through a refiguring of language show us that they are experiencing their situation anew" ("Elements of Style" 9).

"Signifyin" is a practice that goes back to early African culture, but it has been discussed most famously by Henry Louis Gates Jr., who says that it "*is* repetition and revision, or repetition with a signal difference" (xxiv). Gates suggests that "Signifyin" (which he writes with a capital *S* and an absent or parenthetical *g* at the end to distinguish its "free play" from the "order and coherence" implied by the lowercase *s* and its denotative emphases [see Gates 46, 49]) is a form of discursive practice we can see in African-American literature extending back to slave narratives. To "Signify" is to mimic or echo dominant discourse, but to repeat it in a subversive way that lets the (knowing) listener or reader understand how that discourse is being mimicked, undermined, reinscribed, revised, and reused for purposes that may run counter to the original, authoritarian intent. Gates writes, "It is this principle of repetition and difference, this practice of intertextuality, which has been so crucial to the black vernacular forms of Signifyin(g), jazz—and even its antecedents, the blues, the spirituals, and ragtime—and which is the source of my trope for black intertextuality" (64). Analyzing the relation of Gates's sense of "Signifyin" to Parks, Haike Frank explains that multiple meanings ensue, "as is the case when a speaker of the black vernacular consciously empties the white signifier of its original white signified, substituting it with a different signified that expresses the black experience" (6). For example, Parks "signifies" on the assassination of Abraham Lincoln by having it performed repeatedly by a black Lincoln in *The America Play*. She "signifies" on many artifacts from racist discourse in *Last Black Man*, such as the "cure for big lips" formula repeated by the Prunes and Prisms character. Louise Bernard explains the connection between Gates's account and Parks's appropriation of jazz composition techniques:

> Parks's larger framework of Signification, or tropological revision— i.e., the way in which a specific trope is repeated with difference between two or more texts [cf. Gates]—mirrors the multilayered equivalents in the jazz composition: (1) *Rep & Rev* within a given tune; (2) the intertextual dynamic between a (European) standard and a jazz riff (for example, Coltrane's rendition of "My Favorite Things"); and (3) the jazz musician's personal riff on another jazz musician's "standard" (for example, the variations of Ellington's "Caravan"). (693)

Similarly, though Parks does not incorporate the blues directly until her later works (e.g., Lincoln's song in *Topdog/Underdog*, the mother as blues singer in *Getting Mother's Body*), the influence of blues structure is relevant from the beginning. Again, the blues line relies on a pattern of repetition and variation; blues songs also are notorious for "signifyin," often in terms of the subversive, sometimes hidden sexual meanings of the lyrics.

Parks uses "rep and rev" to "signify" because the subversive repetition of a line, act, or visual image has a transformative effect while calling the subject repeatedly into memory, often in a ritual fashion. As Dixon says, "In performance a subtle phrase or gesture can, with repetition, be transformed into a larger metaphor" (58); in *Last Black Man*, for example, the image of the Black Man moving his hands recurs—with variations—and becomes one of the images of the figure's movements between death and life. Another way that Parks "signifies" is in her use of repeated or choruslike lines; one thinks of such passages as "Emergency, Oh, emergency . . ." from *America Play* (160), "This is the death of the last black man in the whole entire world" from the play by that name, and "Diggidy-diggidy-diggidy-diggidy" (3) from *Venus*. The choral repetitions give the play a musical structure that evokes elements of African oral tradition, worksongs, and churchlike call-and-response. Parks remarks, "The verses contain the information or meat, the choruses the fun, the fat, the gravy. The power of the chorus comes not from the presentation of new information but from its repeating" (Jacobus 1632–33).

The tradition of "signifyin" in African-American performance can be witnessed not only in the musical forms of jazz and the blues, but also in the popular entertainment forms of burlesque, minstrelsy, and vaudeville, which sometimes featured whites performing in blackface, but which also existed in black performances dating back to minstrel troupes formed just after the Civil War (and which could be seen in late-twentieth-century versions such as "Showtime at the Apollo"). Leslie W. Lewis reminds us that "black performance history begins from within and by signifying on the racial stereotypes of blackface minstrelsy" (56). The vaudeville-minstrelsy form resurfaces frequently in Parks's works, from Lucius and Mare's routines in *Betting on the Dust Commander*, to Ham's "stump speech" in *Last Black Man*, to the whiteface version of *Our American Cousin* in *The America Play*, to the Negro Resurrectionist as "interlocutor" in *Venus*, to the Ma and Pa Kettle routine that the brothers Lincoln and Booth do in *Topdog/Underdog*. Parks is fond of not only the comic timing that comes from vaudeville-style dialogue, but also of the signifying in these forms that often comes from punning and other forms of wordplay.

While Parks draws upon these traditional forms, like many postmodern theater artists (e.g., Charles Mee, Lee Breuer, Robert Wilson, and others), she incorporates mixed media in her works. Early pieces such as *Imperceptible Mutabilities in the Third Kingdom* and *Betting on the Dust Commander* feature slides; *Last Black Man* and *The America Play* have figures on television; productions of *Venus* have featured mixed-media historical representations of Saartjie Baartman; the Know Theatre Tribe's 2006 production of *In the Blood* played film versions of Hester during the characters' monologues about their encounters with her. Playing with these forms, especially photographs, allows Parks to comment on the dubious truth-telling of such representations (though her plays make no claims to truth). Exceeding the boundaries of what theater is "supposed" to include, she brings in alternative visual forms and texts to create a Brechtian distancing from the plot and characters in favor of competing, more critical forms of scrutiny.

Her characterization, again like Brecht's, prevents audience members from immersing themselves in the characters as if they were real. A "character" in Parks is not grounded in psychological realism, Stanislavskian biographical motivation, or emotional affect. To call her figures "characters" would be "an injustice," Parks says; instead, "[T]hey are *figures, figments, ghosts, roles, lovers* maybe, *speakers* maybe, *shadows, slips, players* maybe, maybe *someone else's pulse*" (12). This is not to say that they lack complexity; they may be overlaid with the historical resonance of a real or fictional figure from the past (such as Venus in the play by that name, or Hester in *In the Blood*) or with the psychological complexity of conflict (as the brothers Booth and Lincoln are in *Topdog/Underdog*). However, it would be accurate to describe Parks's characters as "figures." Often they do not resemble a person who could be real but instead represent an idea or political or historical concept. The figures Lots of Grease and Lots of Pork and Yes and Greens Black-Eyed Peas Cornbread in *Last Black Man* represent soul food traditions, and (as will be discussed in the chapter "Choral Explorations") part of the pleasure and challenge of the work is figuring out how to embody these figures on stage. W. B. Worthen argues that Parks's "figments" (as she calls them) are also "figments of the idea of dramatic 'character' itself" (16). Characters may seem to exist both in and out of time, in a Beckettian limbo, as we see for Miss Miss in *Pickling* or Lucius and Mare in *Betting on the Dust Commander*. The same play may present characters on different levels of representation; for example, in *Venus*, the protagonist and the Baron Docteur are both mythical and historical; the Negro Resurrectionist and the Mother-Showman are fictional but three-dimensional; the Bride-to-Be and the other play-within-a-play characters are theatrical and two-dimensional (one production even used puppets to represent them); the circus freaks are exaggerations or abstractions. It is a mistake to claim that Parks has "evolved" into creating psychologically complex characters in later plays such as *Topdog*. Booth and Lincoln fit on a continuum that merges the fictional, the mythical, the historical, and the psychological, and that includes the Foundling Father from her related *America Play*. We should be wary of reviewers' tendency to favor more "believable" or "fleshed out" representations.

Just as she eschews naturalistic or psychological representations of character, Parks is less interested in "plot" than in the theatrical event. With the possible exception of *Topdog/Underdog*, her plays focus more on ritual than on climactic narrative. Indeed, in "Elements of Style," she includes hand-drawn "diagrams" for several of her plays, using mock-mathematical "equations": for example, the picture for *Last Black Man* is of the measurements of a coffin, with instructions to "find the volume of the solid" and then to "find the half-life" (13). If these "equations" are difficult to understand or seem parodic, that is precisely the point; Parks resists what she calls the "bad math" of "clarity" (14). Referring to *Last Black Man*, she has said that "on stage, as in physics, an event doesn't have to be big to be a big deal. In the theater, someone can simply turn their hand palm up and that is an event" (Solomon 79).

Another defining feature of Parks's texts is her vision of time and space. Time is linked to repeatability and to the "rep and rev"; as S. E. Wilmer puts it, "Parks has replaced the 'aura' of historical event or epoch with the notion of time as infinitely repeatable" (448). Wilmer also points out that for Parks, "[t]he stage space is simultaneously historical, contemporary, and imaginary" (444). Space in the theater is defined in part by the way that actors move within it. "Plays are about space to me," says Parks (Jiggetts 309). She provides few stage directions for her actors: "The action goes in the line of dialogue instead of always in a pissy set of parentheses" ("Elements of Style" 15). Often, therefore, stage action is embodied through performative language; in other words, it is possible to figure out what a character is *doing* by paying close attention to what he or she is *talking about doing*, such as when we hear the patter that accompanies the three-card monte deal in *Topdog/Underdog*.

In Parks silence becomes a strategic and intentional device, as in Beckett, although she is not particularly interested in the pause as a unit of silence. Short silences in her works are indicated as "rests."

She comments, "'Rest' is actually a great word. It's musical. And having the word 'rest' over and over and over to indicate every single place where the character takes a little break in between paragraphs of speech is perfect" (Pearce 26). It is the more complicated rest, the "spell," which has become one of Parks's most notable and talked-about stylistic elements, and a consistent challenge for actors performing her work (although a "spell" doesn't manifest itself as effectively in print, its unique presentation in the text does force the reader to slow down). The character, says Parks, " is not speaking but is taking up space on the page and is taking up time on the page and must take up space and time similarly on the stage" (Drukman 70).

In a "spell," the text provides the names of the characters without accompanying dialogue:

Lincoln
Booth
Lincoln
Booth

Parks notes that in such sequences, "This is a place where the figures experience their pure true simple state. While no 'action' or 'stage business' is necessary, directors should fill this moment as they best see fit" ("Elements of Style" 16). Looking at a daguerreotype, or imagining that "the planets are aligning, and as they move we hear the music of their spheres," is a way to feel the inside of a spell: "A spell is a place of great (unspoken) emotion. It's also a place for an emotional transition" (16–17). The term *spell*, of course, conjures up multiple meanings: it is simultaneously a moment of magic or hypnosis, a spelling out of how two characters are feeling, and a folk idiom for an indefinite period of time (as in "sit down and rest a spell") or for a trance or illness ("she's having one of her spells"). An audience may or may not be made aware of when spells are taking place, depending in part on what the actors do during one of them.

Jennifer Johung's detailed discussion of the spells in *Venus* provides a way of looking at their function in Parks's work as a whole. Johung is captivated by the unorthodox look of the spells on the pages of the play text, and the complicated transition from page and stage that readers, spectators, directors, and performers must undertake. Johung suggests that the spells may be imagined as a kind of musical notation, with the names of the figures analogous to notes:

> If we can imagine the names of a spell as musical notes, then we can conceptualize the space of spell as a vertical spread or chord—with all names/notes sounded together—gesturing toward a horizontal progression through time—with one name/note sounded after another. (51–52)

Johung explains that Parks's spells on the page allow us to imagine the transition to their embodiment in *performance*, especially as a character's identity is shaped in physical relation to another character.

A final textual intervention that teases our assumptions about page and stage is Parks's inclusion of footnotes. One is reminded of her modernist predecessor, T. S. Eliot, with his notes to *The Wasteland*; many postmodernist authors have played with the borders between notes as academic information and notes as fanciful or parodic intervention (see, for example, works by David Foster Wallace or Dave Eggers, or perhaps Vladimir Nabokov's entire *Pale Fire*). Of course, a footnote in a play text is not normally part of the performance. As Elam and Rayner remark about *The America Play*, "[T]he footnotes play with the status of the peripheral text as a sign for marginalized experience. Where are those footnotes in performance? Like the exclusions of history, they are on the side" ("Echoes" 186). *Imperceptible Mutabilities in the Third Kingdom* includes footnotes in part 3 ("Open House") that provide information ranging from a coop sales term to the history of slavery. In *Last Black Man*, Parks adds note numbers without corresponding texts (or are they mathematical exponents?) to the genealogical stump speech offered by Ham. The footnotes in *The America Play* (discussed at greater length in the chapter "Resurrecting Lincoln") become, in the play text, part of the dialogue between "truths" and tale-telling in American history; Parks mixes "real" and invented or speculative information. As Kurt Bullock puts it in his insightful discussion, "Parks toys with the traditional conventions of endnotes by demonstrating them to be both factual and fictional, legitimating and problematizing" (80–81). In *Venus*, finally, the notes are incorporated in the performance, as the Negro Resurrectionist narrates them as part of the series of "Historical Extracts" about Saartjie Baartman that he gives the audience; here, the spectators are confronted with the question of whether "research" on the Venus Hottentot tells the whole story (see further discussion in the chapter "Anatomizing *Venus*").

Traditionally, notes serve two purposes: they bolster the "authority" of a text by providing documentation, and they are a repository for information that may not fit in the body of a discussion. Parks is interested in both of these aspects: at times, her notes show the play as a process—one that involves mediation and labor on the part of the author—and she juxtaposes real and imagined information as an indication that history (with its exclusions, especially of African-Americans) is predicated on *narratives* that may not tell the "whole" story. Thus, notes are also a way of working liminally with the play text; they provide a kind of ghost-voice from the playwright as creator, but they also (in the plays other than *Venus*) hover in the margins of the performance. The notes, like so many of Parks's stylistic trademarks, legitimize (the playwright did Research), mock-legitimize, and "ill-legitimize": in other words, they deflate and mock, or perhaps bastardize, the sacrosanct play text, history play, or historical narrative.

Telling is suspect, Parks seems to say, and genealogies are by nature discontinuous because their parts have been dis-membered.

Elements of Style: Early Plays

*Betting on the Dust Commander,
Pickling, Devotees in the Garden of Love*

In the late 1980s and early 1990s, Parks began working on several pieces that would show signs of what became her characteristic style. Two of them, *Imperceptible Mutabilities in the Third Kingdom* and *The Death of the Last Black Man in the Whole Entire World*, developed into longer works and will be discussed in the following chapter. Three of the early dramas that remained brief works are the topic of this chapter. *Betting on the Dust Commander, Pickling*, and *Devotees in the Garden of Love* are fascinating on several levels. They show the strong influence of modernist writers such as Gertrude Stein and Samuel Beckett. Moreover, they develop many of the themes (such as memory/dis-membering, resurrection, photography and other media portrayals, and distorted relationships) that would surface in her later works.

Betting on the Dust Commander

Parks first produced and directed *Betting on the Dust Commander* in 1987, on a shoestring budget, at the Gas Station, a bar in the East Village in New York ("I was the happiest girl in New York City," she recalled [Parks, "An Evening"]). In 1990, Liz Diamond directed a production for Company One in Hartford, Connecticut, and again in

| 23

1991 for New York's Working Theater. The premise is simple: a couple, Lucius and Mare, reminisce and argue about their past, bringing up their childhood, their relationship, Lucius's devotion to horse racing, and the consequences of death. Some would call the play a maddening one, but perhaps that is precisely the point. The text begins with an epigraph from Gertrude Stein's *The Making of Americans* that helps to explain what Parks is up to:

> Repeating then is in every one, in every one their being and their
> feeling and their way of realizing everything and every one
>   comes out
> of them in repeating . . .
> Slowly every one in continuous repeating, to their
>   minutest variation,
> comes to be clearer to some one.

In Stein's work, repetition is seen as both structurally and ontologically inevitable, as if we make our way through the world by means of repetition, yet the process evolves into variations, as if an end point happens in spite of all. We can see a clear link between Stein's idea of repetition and Parks's "rep and rev," which, as was discussed in the preceding chapter, is drawn from the aesthetics of jazz improvisation. More directly than any of her other works, *Dust Commander* depends on the effects of repetition to make its dramatic points. In her "Elements of Style" essay, Parks comments that in this play, "the 'climax' could be the accumulated weight of the repetition—a residue that, like city dust, stays with us" (10)—and dust itself is one of the repeated images. Rep and rev forms the structure of the work, but it also represents the existential situation of its two characters, Lucius and Mare.

The first scene (scene A) is a flashback to Lucius and Mare's wedding day. Although an audience expects to see characters present onstage or to enter immediately when a play begins, Parks opens audaciously by presenting us instead with a double-frame slide show of these two characters in their wedding outfits, while we hear the actors speaking through offstage microphones. In this way, Parks introduces immediately the idea of simulation, of our stories, memories, and photographs of the past as replications that allow us to enact a *version* of the past that is not an authoritative historical documentation of it. Indeed, Lucius's first line to Mare is, "Make the alteration?" (75). We come to realize that he is referring to the substitution of plastic flowers for real ones in the church (because the real ones make him sneeze). This alteration, this substitution of the simulated for the real, suggests, as do the photographs, the effort to freeze a moment in time (a theme to which Parks will return in *Pickling* and many other works). The value of the simulation is determined by its realness, staying power, and ability to fool people (i.e., dis-simulation); as Mare says to Lucius, "Expensive plastics got the real look to em, Lucius. Expensive plastics got uh smell. Expensive plastics will last a lifetime but nobodyll know, Lucius. Nobody knows" (75).

As the second scene begins and we see Lucius and Mare on stage, Parks develops the key tropes of the play. The first of these is that Lucius and Mare have a childlike relationship: the scene begins with Mare crossing her eyes and Lucius warning her that her eyes are going to get stuck. Thus begins the "stuck-that-way-forever" (83) imagery that pervades the play and is evinced later in a discussion of rigor mortis. This early exchange about eye-crossing also shows the habitual teasing between the two characters, almost as if they were brother and sister; at one point Mare wails, "Mmtellin Mama!" (77), though shortly afterward we find out that the mother is probably dead: "Mammas with her Maker" (79). The daughter is dependent upon the dead mother and has never really grown up. The implication is that the two characters were joined together so young that by now they have "outgrowed of our twin cots" (78). They seem to have tried having sex or making a baby one time only, but when Mare suggests, "We cud have wee ones, Luki . . . Didnt make nothing thuh first time maybe we could try again," Lucius resists, responding that it is "[m]essy" (79).

Another trope, established in scene A when the flowers make Lucius sneeze, is a continual emphasis on sneezing, coughing, crying, and nose-blowing; Lucius even attempts to instruct Mare on how to blow her nose properly. She says she has been practicing:

"Didnt have no snots at first, Lucius. At first didnt have no tears" (78). The preoccupation with sneezing and the like is connected to dust as a central image. In Lucius's view, Mare doesn't get the big picture, and dust is an example: "Thuh little things done thundered you by in one big pack . . . Dust is little bits of dirt, Mare . . . that— fuzzicate theirselves together n make dusts" (79–80). The attention to sneezing and sniffling reinforces the characters' preoccupation with bodily functions, and allows Parks to indulge her fondness for punning. Mare says that her nose is "ssuh hood ornament" that she used to "win" Lucius, and his response suggests that she did so just barely, "[b]y uh nose" (77, 78).

Lucius's phrase also calls attention to another trope (one that echoes the title of the play): horse racing (of course, Mare's name is linked to a horse, as is her constant snuffling). Lucius tells Mare that he has to leave to catch the "3:10 race at The Churchill" (77) and implies a religious devotion to the track, referring to it as his "Church date" (78). The images of sneezing and horse racing come together when Mare tells how she met Lucius:

> I was cleaning your table . . . You laughed at my nose. I was dusting— snucch—feather duster—yellow feathers—snucch—you laughed at my nose—snucch—the first horse won by the nose, remember? It was dusty. You sneezed—snucch—your hunch was the dust. Dust Commanders running today you sniffed—snuccch—by the nose she'll win I said. Dusty Commander won by a nose, remember? (78)

Lucius says that he still carries the clipping (and he shows it to Mare) of the time that he got his picture in the paper because he bet thirty-five cents on Dust Commander (winner of the Kentucky Derby in 1970). He won at 100:1 odds: "Wreath in the winnin circle—real flowers" (81), as opposed to the plastic flowers of his wedding day. Lucius seems determined to relive these glory days by going back to the track every day (a cycle of repetition), where, he says, everyone recognizes him by his Bermuda shorts and his hat.

As the two characters talk about Dust Commander's comeback, Mare refers to the event as a "regular glue factory resurrection" (80). Fascination with the dead coming back to life pervades Parks's plays, from the Black Man who dies over and over again, to Venus resurrected, to Lincoln shot again and again. As in so many of these works, there is a desire to keep or preserve something that has died; Mare and Lucius talk about the gold budgie he bought her that Mare wanted to hold onto after its death. Lucius says, "Gived you uh ziplocked bag for it. Iffen you was gonna keep it under your pillow you had tuh use thuh bag" (80). When Mare responds that animals shouldn't be kept in plastic or they can't breathe, and Lucius protests that it was dead anyway, Mare retorts that the budgie was "[b]reathing in my dreams" (81). Her later image of the icebox that needs defrosting calls to mind the icebox imagery in *Pickling:* it embodies the constant urge to freeze or preserve the past. And being frozen also evokes the word that Mare and Lucius try to remember for what happens after somebody dies, as Lucius says he fears getting stuck:

MARE. Hold thooe iced cubes for me, Luki.
LUCIUS. Ssscold. Stretched out tuh win. Hope they stretch me out like that. Hope they get me in thuh home stretch fore I get all stuck up: arms this way, elbows funny, knees knocking, head all wrong. Waas that word—that word for the dead-stuck? Mare, the dead-stuck?
MARE. Riggamartin's.
LUCIUS. Riggamartin's. Yep. Hope they get me afore I go Riggamartin's. Ssscold. (81–82)

Lucius's statement that it's cold makes Mare go on to insist that for this reason, he shouldn't go to the track in his Bermuda shorts. Her offer to wash and iron them causes Lucius to reminisce about their wedding pictures and to ask how long ago that was; Mare responds, ambiguously, that it was "[o]ne year long ago" (82). The characters themselves seem to be frozen in time, trapped (as we shall soon see) in a cycle of repetition, a kind of life-in-death.

The image of repetition also shows itself as Lucius tells Mare a story about another woman he met at the track whose situation seems to match hers (a bit like the famous anecdote wherein a couple figures out that they may or may not be married to each other in Eugène Ionesco's absurdist play *The Bald Soprano*). Lucius talks about his conversation with the woman that includes a discussion of how he keeps his Bermuda shorts clean. He says to Mare, "She was like you like you in every respect. Looked like you spoked like made eyes like you coulda bccn you was you. I thought. I thought" (82). Just as in *The Bald Soprano,* wherein the deduction that the couple is married may turn out to be wrong, Lucius seems to be referring to Mare but also claims that he is talking about a different woman, adding that the woman now is dead (or at least has exited from his life): "She passed, you know. Shes got all the questions now" (82). The status of this other woman is indeterminate: was she Mare, unrecognized by Lucius, or was she indeed another woman? Did they have a flirtation or affair? Parks enacts her theme of identity as uncertain, a sense in which one's very being is always at risk of duplication or erasure. Lucius is confused about who the woman was because he lives in a (dramatic) universe in which repetition seems to provide reassurance, but it prevents recognition.

Like Vladimir and Estragon in Beckett's *Waiting for Godot,* Lucius keeps insisting that he is about to go but does not leave; like the crossed eyes, the characters seem to be stuck forever. More than that, the play at this point (83–84) begins to recycle the previous conversations, with variations: this is Parks's "rep and rev." Just as the horses run "every day at 3:10" (83), the couple seems to have the same conversation over and over. They reenact, for instance, the exchange about blowing Mare's nose, and Mare's anecdote about meeting Lucius for the first time while she was cleaning tables with her yellow feather duster. Interestingly, Lucius's praise for Mare's blowing her nose seems to acknowledge the repetition: "Gets easier the second time. Easier n easier till sseffortless" (84). Yet they seem to have had the same conversation more than twice. Considered in this light, the reiterated remarks about Dust Commander becoming a "glue factory resurrection" (86) and having "gone forth n multiplied" (87) refer to the horse's figurative resurrection and replication every time their dialogue reoccurs. This is a metadramatic image as well, since the repetition of the repetition takes place every time the piece is rehearsed or performed.

The play's closing scene is a rep and rev of the slide show that comprised the opening: again, Lucius' and Mare's voices are miked from offstage as we see the same slide show we saw before. Our sense of making the "alterations" now includes the feeling not only of revision and correction, but of the slight changes within the frame of repetition. We don't get the impression that Lucius and Mare are condemned to repeat themselves until they get it "right." Rather, Parks implies that everyday life itself evokes this process of—to requote the Stein epigraph—"every one in continuous repeating" (75).

Pickling

> V. Will you never have done? [*Pause.*] Will you never have done . . . revolving it all?
>
> —Samuel Beckett, *Footfalls* (*Collected Shorter Plays* 240)

> . . , just one of those things you kept making up to keep the void out just another of those old tales to keep the void from pouring in on top of you the shroud.
>
> —Beckett, *That Time* (*Collected Shorter Plays* 230)

Parks once said of Samuel Beckett, "[H]e just seems so black to me" (qtd. by Jonathan Kalb in "Remarks on Parks 1," 2). It is hard to imagine Parks's 1988 play *Pickling*, a monologue spoken by a character named Miss Miss, without thinking of Beckett. As in so many of his short later plays (*Footfalls, Rockaby, Not I,* etc.) the speaker and protagonist is an eccentric older woman who seems to have stepped apart from life and become isolated (sometimes, in Beckett, an old man is the speaker, as in *Eh Joe* or *Krapp's Last Tape*). *Pickling* was first performed as a radio play in 1990 by New American Radio, and it is worth remembering that some of Beckett's short pieces (such as *Rough for Radio* or *Words and Music*) were also produced in this medium. As in Beckett, the language is densely poetic, full of neologisms and repetitions that gradually paint a picture for the audience. The most prolific director of the stage version of the play has been Allison Eve Zell, who has done five sequential productions: at the Harlem Summer Arts Festival in 1998, the Lincoln Center Directors

Lab at HERE Arts Center in 1999, the Mint Space and Joe's Pub at the Public Theater in 2000 and 2001, and the Cherry Lane Theatre in 2002. In the stage version, again like Beckett, Parks makes a minimalist but crucial use of the set and props. One might think of the gray urns from which the heads of the speakers protrude in *Play* (*Pickling*, as we shall see, is also concerned with vessels), the rocking chair in *Rockaby*, or the banana and tape recorder in *Krapp's Last Tape*. Finally, although Parks' aesthetic and historical interests are ultimately rather different, there are thematic links between this piece and Beckett's similar monologues: both feature characters who are paralyzed with the memories of past points in their lives and seem now, on the brink of death, to be finding some sort of final outburst or reprieve through the act of narration.

The speaker in *Pickling* is named Miss Miss. She has much in common with the elderly women who populate Beckett's late monologues, but she also an instance of the African- American trope of the slightly crazed older "church lady" who never married and has been accepted into the community for who she is. In her memoir *Bone Black*, bell hooks writes about such women:

> Every Sunday Miss Erma sits on the third pew. No one ever sits in her place. Even if she is late it is there waiting—a space large enough for two people. She is short and plump like our Big Mama. She walks with a cane, wears funny hats. I do not want to grow up to be a woman who wears funny hats. . . . We noticed her not because of her funny hats, not even because of the way that she has a special place reserved for her but because she is old, because she has long been a member of this church. She is one of the church founders. . . . We notice her because during the sermon, just as the preacher is reaching the point at which what he says reaches into our hearts so that we feel it pressed against the passionate beating—she screams out in a loud and piercing voice, one long sentence. . . . Who can remember when this short plump woman wearing face powder that made it appear her skin was covered in ash first spoke to me. (43–44)

Miss Miss is well educated—she gives us a series of parodic etymological links from the French *passé* to German to African dialect to English (94)—but she has also removed herself from the rest of the

Jaye Austin Williams in *Pickling*, director Allison Eve Zell. HERE Arts
Center, New York City. Photo by Barry Steele.

world, having decided "never need to go out outside is overwhelming
and too much. Havent been out since" (94). Her name conjures up
both the "old maid" who is still a Miss; she has "missed" the boat
somehow, missed out on the rest of life.

She begins by singing part of a hymn to us—"I wiped his
brow . . ." (93), and she tells us that her mother would have her sing
for guests: "In my home . . . They come for miles. To see me. I sang!
Beautifully. Accompany myself with my jars. Hadnt been done
before" (94). Her song was "a prell-yude. One uh them pray-lude
songs" to begin her "farewell performance," in which she was to
recite "uh short drama in ten short pages" (95). *Pickling* itself, which
also begins with the song and is a "short drama," of the same length,
seems to have become the recitation with which she is now left. As
with Beckett's characters, we get the impression that she has been
rehearsing parts of it over and over for many years.

After her hymn, she plays with the sound of a word (much like
Krapp with the word "spool" in Beckett), in this case "taut" (93). The

Jaye Austin Williams in *Pickling,* director Allison Eve Zell. The Mint Space, New York City. Photo by Andrew Kern.

word is onomatopoetic, imitating the sound of something that has been tightened. It is the beginning of the play's images of immobility and enclosure ("Taut flesh," the icebox [93]) that move to the jars ("The lid on this one is very tight. Taut" [95]) and are the pivotal prop and metaphor of the piece. As a death image, tautness, or rigidity, invokes the rigor mortis ("Riggamartins") of *Betting on the Dust Commander*. As often in Parks's work, it is also a pun on the word "taught": Miss Miss's speech is a series of *mis*-teachings—some of which she seems to have learned from her mother—that she is now "teaching" to the audience.

Miss Miss's opening mention of the icebox sets up the idea of the coffinlike preservation that she will connect to her collection of jars. Its door handle was "[s]oiled with mothers milk" that "never comes clean" (93). The ambiguity of the possessive in "mothers" is interesting, for we don't know whether she is referring to her own breast milk (did she lose a baby?) or her mother's; the latter seems more likely, as she discusses her mother's death. She admonishes herself to "put the milk back in the jar" (94) so that it will turn into "Powdermilk. Dust. Then for guests we will have to reactivate. Rise up from thuh dead" (94). Birth (mother's milk) and death are thus conflated, as they are increasingly in the piece (and throughout Parks's works). This idea of saving something to "reactivate" it previews the digging and resurrection in her later plays; "reactivating" something for "guests" is also a metadramatic image insofar as the guests present are the listening audience for a spoken piece that gets "reactivated" whenever it is performed.

Beckett's elderly figures often recall a lost love or mangled relationship, and the same is true for Miss Miss. She tells us about Charles, a lifeguard neighbor, and mentions repeatedly that he had "[s]uch bicepts" (95). When she was younger, Miss Miss apparently played the jars as a musical instrument to entertain guests, and recalls that "[e]ach jar has a distinctly different sound" (94). We gradually realize that she is now using her collection of jars to save memories, some of which are material artifacts and some of which are figurative remnants of her past. She shows us a jar of sand from the day that she met Charles at the beach—"I saved sand from that day.

Uh whole jar full. Had tuh dig under thuh snow tuh get at it" (95). According to Miss Miss, he saved her life that day by pulling her from the ice: "He pulled me out and blew—his lips on my lips—a professional savior" (97). She refers to Charles several times as a savior, making the lifeguard a religious redeemer, and she calls him a "tanned and laughing Moses" who "would show me thuh key to thuh kingdom" (97). That is, she claims that on Thursdays (his evening off) Charles came to her house and they engaged in sex: "He is my guest. The cup with his lips mark. Here. The sand from his bare feet. In this one. His wind: breath; gas. The prophylactic: our love object. Thuh light likes this one. Our love. Don't open it Miss Miss" (95).

Parks takes the familiar modern tactic of mixing memory and desire, but gives it an additional, metatheatrical-Beckettian twist. Although we are not sure that Miss Miss actually had the experiences she tells us about, she presents the contents of the jars as "evidence." The purported contents are not things that one would normally save, nor are they necessarily "real." Just as literature preserves, contains, freezes the past for reactivation when desired (see Keats's "Ode on a Grecian Urn"), the jars as prop become a physical manifestation of the urge to preserve and narrate that past. This interest in the artifact becomes a crucial part of Parks's later plays (cf. *Last Black Man, The America Play, Venus*). Kimberly Dixon, taking a different approach, sees a connection between the pickled jar contents and "the inevitable performative dormancy in Parks's written notation of her plays" (65). Dixon implies that the texts of the plays are waiting to be opened and enacted, in order to have the full power of their contents released.

Miss Miss recalls an "x-change" that she had with Charles in which they discussed "thuh great-nigger-queen-bee-who-lives-at-thuh-center-of-Mars"; their disagreement came when "[h]e said 'center.' I said "Uh little off" (95). Although the text never explains what this figure represents, it is yet another alternate godhead; her insistence that this figure be a "little off" center resembles the interest in off-centering (both on stage and in terms of ex-centricity) of Beckett's monologue characters. She and Charles part company, however, when Miss Miss shows him the parts of her mother that she has saved: she says, "Her photograph went over well enough. Only show one side of a person the pictures do" (95–96). The macabre image we get (though we don't know for sure that it is to be taken literally) is of the "parts" of the dead mother that Miss Miss has collected ("Kept her red gums too. Pickledem" [96]). She says that Charles laughed when he saw the mother's picture ("I have his laugh. Right here: Oh oh ha heup: Charles" [96]), but accused her of practicing voodoo when he witnessed the jar collection containing the dead mother. Her comment, "Didnt find fault with her picture but did mind her parts isnt that always thuh way" (96), speaks not just to the moment being described but to her experience of sexuality, fraught with the notion that the man prefers the outward image to the down-and-dirty existence of "parts."

Miss Miss is suffused with physical memories of her mother, and her conflation of herself and her mother makes sense if we take into account her statement,"They say that 'a woman's mother is what— 'the woman'll bee" (96). The spelling of *be* invokes the queen bee mentioned earlier, a sort of matriarch of the universe, or at least of Miss Miss's universe. Miss Miss seems to be haunted by the moment of her mother's death, reenacting it continually in her mind. The mother "was on her way out to let out the dog" (97)—the unexpected exit of death itself is enacted in the process of an exit that never gets completed. The description of the mother's fall is fraught with images of death and after: "Standing at the threshold with the doorhandle in her hand she just—crumbled—. Puddle of her own pickling surrounds her wig like a halo" (97). This obsessive recall of the moment places Miss Miss herself, surrounded by her jar collection, as pickled or frozen in time. In a sense, she will replicate (or has already begun to replicate) the death of her mother: "she lies there quietly there thinking about her life until she stops thinking no more life to think about no more:—cold. Oh" (97).

In the final sequence of the play, Miss Miss changes her previous stories by introducing a new element, saying that she will now tell "the truth" (and it's worth noting that here, *the* is not spelled *thuh* as it is elsewhere). She recalls that in the summers, she and her mother would spend their time pickling beets, canning many jars. When her mother would leave the house to get her hair color touched up ("when mother went out her roots" [97]), Miss Miss would stay and look at the jars in satisfaction: "there were no empty jars you had your beets thats what you had and you had a full life and your beets and noempty jars" (97). It turned out, though, that Charles saw the jars, and for those "[e]ighteen Thursdays," he would sneak into the house and consume the beets: "Gobblin thuh beets on his Thursdays. Smackin lips wipin lips on his wrist" (97). What we never know, then, is whether the previous stories about Charles saving her and about their supposed love affair are true, or whether the "truth" is that his consumption of her juicy red beets was what took place instead.

We are indeed given to understand, though, that this is the source of the jars Miss Miss has and that what Charles was doing was "[e]mptying my jars. Mines. Something tuh re-member you by" (97–98). The play closes with a negation of all her previous claims and accumulations: "from thuh river we float out tuh sea. Nothin tuh carry along. Nothing saved. No mementoes.—No saviors—all left. Gone out" (98). She is describing the state of death, the condition under which there is no more hope of preservation. Her last words combine a final glimmer of sexuality with imagery of murder or suicide: "I told him to do it in here . . . Like steeel he was. Hee! Begin: Steal uhway. Glide-it uhcross. Oh. Warm steal. Oh. Warm. Warm. Oh: To thuh worms. To thuh worms. To thuh worms" (98; last line has no period). Like the characters in Beckett's monologues, then, one cannot say for sure whether the central figure is thus addressing us after death or in a state that anticipates death. The final metamorphosis from "warm" to "worms" suggests an acceptance, perhaps even a welcoming, of this final condition. As in so many of Parks's works (cf. *Last Black Man*, *Venus*, *Topdog/Underdog*, and her novel *Getting Mother's Body*), death is on the horizon from the very beginning. In *Pickling*, she entertains the images of preservation and memory that will become prevalent in later work, where she also insists on possibilities of (failed) resurrection.

Devotees in the Garden of Love

In interviews given at the time of the premiere of *Venus*, Parks mentioned frequently that she had wanted to write a play about love. Looking at the works of her earlier career, we see that *Venus* is far from the first play on this subject; indeed, one might say that *Betting on the Dust Commander* and *Pickling* are plays about, respectively, the successes and failures of love, warped though their versions of them may be. In *Devotees in the Garden of Love* (written in 1991–92, first performed in 1992 at the Humana Festival of the Actors Theatre of Louisville), Parks takes on this subject even more explicitly.

The title conjures up a painting, and as she does so often, Parks begins with a tableau. In this case, a young woman, George, and a little old lady in a wheelchair, Lily, are in the titular garden on a hilltop. Steven Drukman remarks that the two characters remind him of Hamm and Clov in Beckett's *Endgame* (70). Adding to the Beckettian feel, both women are attired in wedding dresses. Lily evokes not only the protagonist in Beckett's *Rockaby*, but also, of course, Estelle Havisham in Dickens's *Great Expectations*. *Devotees* is also a play about war and about watching. Comments Parks:

> In *Devotees* black people are watching something we never see. We can assume that it's just a bunch of black people having war. We can assume that by extension because we never see the war. We are told about it but we are never told, but the two black women on the hilltop are watching the war. (Jiggetts 313)

As the play begins, George is practicing her French conversation while Lily clucks disapprovingly that in her day "uh woman spoke of her table. And that was all" (135). George, ignoring her, fantasizes about love, pretending to address "Monsieur Amour" (135). As they do throughout the play, the two women are spying down the hillside, using a lorgnette and then binoculars—"BO-NOCKS!" (136)—to comment on the action unfolding below. They form a reciprocal to the play's audience, which is looking up (in most stage and set designs) at the two characters. George speaks repeatedly about

Esther Scott and Margarette Robinson in *Devotees in the Garden of Love*, director Oskar Eustis. Actors Theatre of Louisville. Photo by Richard Trigg.

Madame Odelia Pandahr, a yenta or matchmaker of sorts (the cast list describes her as a "panderer" [134]) who seems to have been enlisted to help George select a husband from the throng below. Initially not understanding who Madame Pandahr is, Lily is appalled that some "huzzy" (135) is down among the men. George explains that Madame is "monitoring thuh situation play by play" and that her efforts, while known formerly as matchmaking, are now to be considered a form of "reportage" (136). Madame's role, then, is caught up in the idea of watching and being watched, of the desired woman as both spectator and spectacle. George tells Lily:

> Madame Odelia Pandahr says that because all the eyes of the world are on the heart of the bride-who'll-be's heart thuh bride-who'll-be's heart thus turns inward, is given to reflection and in that way becomes an eye itself. Seeing inward to examine her most deepest thoughts and feelings and seeing outward tuh give her form and grace

thatll guide her in the her most natural selection, that is, her choice of suitors. (136)

George's words may be read in several ways. To some extent, they are a parody of the rhetoric one finds in women's magazines, in articles that promise them the transcendence available through the act of falling in love and achieving bridehood; perhaps George has internalized these sentiments. Her emphasis on the heart becoming an "eye," with the pun on "I," implies the seeking of identity through the approval of others, through the act of being *seen*. But it is also striking that this character of the "bride-who'll-be" later becomes the Bride-to-Be in the play-within-the-play of *Venus*. In that piece, the character's identity is so caught up in impending- bride status that she lacks a name of her own. Subsuming her own desires to those of her fiancé, the Bride-to-Be disguises herself as the Hottentot Venus because she knows that he desires the exoticism and sexuality that a virgin fiancée does not possess. The bride-to-be in both plays is a commodity, as much a prisoner of the institution of marriage and its concomitant expectations as a willing player in the game of love, perhaps because she doesn't know any better.

The literal battle for George's affections begins, officially, when she drops her hankie as Madame Pandahr has instructed her to do. Lily seems to relish watching the ensuing fights among the suitors, and cheers them on as if she were watching professional wrestling (though her language evokes baby boomer children's games): "Sweet Bejesus answer my prayers looks like ThatOne done sunked ThisOnes battleship rockum sockum rockum sockum" (137). She admonishes George to put the French away because it's "in uh different time zone" and to use their "hometown lingo." Once she finally gets George to pay attention to the spectacle, George falls into the expected jargon with a blurred version of the national anthem: "Rockets red blare at 2 oclock, Mama Lily. Makes my heart sing" (138). She begins to conflate the idea of devotion (in love), which she says is their word, with patriotic jingles: "We will hold fast unto thuh death. We will not come all asunder. We wont flinch" (138).

George and Lily discuss George's past successes at finishing school, where she learned how to set a table and plan a dinner party, and graduated at the top of her class. The humor or irony comes from the blasé way in which, in the midst of reminiscing about social niceties, they remark that in the battle of the suitors there has been "uh decapitation," "[m]ajor dismemberment" (another example of Parks's fascination with this term), and "[c]arnage," all resulting in the "prognosis" that George "just may be married in thuh morning" (139). The ease of such a transition comments on the coexistence of fine manners and bloodlust in American culture, and on the gendered roles that encourage this dualism. Like a president who hosts a dinner party while waging a bloody war, we accept violence (in love and war) because we reassure ourselves that we still practice the social niceties. Indeed, the play was written in 1991, the year of the first Gulf War, and Parks seems to have been struck by the war's turning into a mediatized spectacle of so-called patriotism.

Which suitor triumphs seems so unimportant that the two major contenders in the play are named ThisOne and ThatOne (these names anticipate Ham's "family tree" in *Last Black Man*). George thinks the battle will come to a smooth conclusion because it is being conducted in the name of "L-O-V-E" (140). She says, "ThisOne may sever thuh arms and legs off uh all uh ThatOnes troops and those maimed and mismangled arms and legs would riiiise up uhgain and return to their trunks like uh child coming home for supper when thuh triangle bell was rung" (140). As she does so often in her plays (particularly in *Venus*), Parks conflates the literal and the figurative senses of re-membering, both memory and the reassembling of something that has been dis-membered (forgotten, mutilated). Read in an unironic sense, love has the power to join together what no one can put asunder, to paraphrase the traditional marriage ceremony. Reading in the context of George's character, however, we get a troubled misunderstanding of what love is, rendered as depersonalized and violent. In fact, George's words confuse the rhetoric of marriage with the rhetoric of battle: "We will hold fast. Unto thuh death. We will not come out all asunder. We wont flinch. How come? Cuz thuh cause of Love" (140).

Similarly, she takes out her hope chest to practice, with Lily, for an inspection that combines the ritual of the bride being inspected by the groom with a military inspection. The hope chest contains tablecloths, napkins, place settings, breath mints, doilies, bedsprings, bloomers, brassieres—and, amusingly, her "brideshead," which George assures Mama Lily is "intact" because (à la *Pickling*) "[s]eal on thuh jar iduhnt broke izit?" (142). The ultimate item in the hope chest is a television. It takes Lily off guard, for in her day, she says, messengers reported the goings-on of the bride battles. This is followed by a scene of Madame Odelia Pandahr broadcasting live from the battlefront, discussing "this brilliant display this passionate parade . . . the splatterment the dismemberment," which she says can be summed up in the word "Devotion" (144). *Devotion* in this context assumes several forms: religious devotion, the devotion of love, and patriotic devotion. Someone participating in the cause of, or battle for, true love may metaphorically—if not literally—feel that he or she is engaging in an act of such (emotional) violence that it is like a dismemberment. Parks not only literalizes this image but goes one step further and makes it into a media spectacle.

It turns out that Madame Pandahr expects certain gifts from the aforementioned trousseau and hope chest (purportedly to offer to ThisOne and ThatOne, the battling suitors), and George argues with Lily about what she should give away and what she should keep. Lily reiterates (a "rep and rev") that, in her day, the first thing a bride-to-be thought about was her table. Madame Pandahr says that the previously offered items have been accepted and reshaped for use in the battle: the dishtowels have become "shifts for the war captured," and the salad plates have been cut for use as "an impediment to the advancing shoeless enemy" (146–47). The ultimate gift, she says, has been of her jewelry: both suitors "have pinned the baubles to their respective bodies an act which literally transfixes them. Pinned by desire, they are spurred on to new deeds of devotion" (147). Again, by taking traditional metaphors of the suffering caused by love and making them literal, Parks parodies the extremes of romance— which, in this context, don't seem romantic at all, especially given the matter-of-factness with which it is treated by the three women.

In fact, George seems reluctant to give up any more items from her beloved hope chest in service of the battle; once Madame Pandahr promises that she could "finagle a citation of some sort for you" (148), George reluctantly gives up her binoculars. They can now watch the battle on the television instead.

We return to Madame Pandahr broadcasting from the front. Her words about the nature or name of the battle parody contemporary political euphemisms for fighting: "What began some years ago as a skirmish, what some years ago was upgraded to a conflict now has all the trappings of war" (149). She remarks that ThisOne has insisted "the body could and would continue to fight—headless yes headless if necessary and that it did" (149). Again, we see the emphasis on dismemberment, coupled with an overstated chivalric valiance; the knights fighting for love combine with contemporary media rhetoric. In a nighttime lull (there is a rule of no night fighting), George asks if she can have a "pretty" name like Patty instead (151)—and the text of the play, obligingly, changes her name to Patty. She requests that her mother quiz her, and the two of them exchange lines in what seems to be a script of the correct suitor and bride-to-be dialogue; when Lily (doing the part of the suitor) says, "Oh my heart would be the most basest and plainest of rocks if ever you did not move me," Patty, after a couple of false starts, has the correct reply: "My image, Sir, is merely—a reflection in that safe keeping mirror of your heart" (152). The language is a lyrical reminder of courtly exchange, yet if this is a memorized text, it does not express a love from the heart. The trappings and formulas of love can become separated from the feelings themselves.

While they are rehearsing (an example of the rehearsal-within-the-play we see again in such pieces as *Topdog/Underdog*), Madame Pandahr arrives to announce breathlessly that she is ready to present the victor of the battle. Patty and Lily respond excitedly, and then—in a wonderfully anticlimactic moment—Madame Pandahr makes a great flourish and uncovers a head on a platter. "Wheres thuh rest of im, Madame?" asks Patty (153). Madame insists that the victor is "full of love" for her, that his "lips are pursed in a kiss," and that the head, which can be "kept alive by a wealth of technology," is "the place where sit thuh lofty—the lofty-most thoughts. Weve, you could say, done away with thuh base" (154). Patty is disappointed; she keeps asking where the rest of him is and reminds Madame that they were supposed to "fall into eachothers arms" (154). Madame admits that there is some debate over whether the victor is actually ThisOne or ThatOne, but claims that she knows him to be the latter: "I am after all his mother" (155). She prods Patty to lean in close because the head is about to speak, and asks, "Now hows that? Uh happy ending!" Patty responds, "Oooh. Mama? He said: 'Be Mine'" (155).

If the play ended there, it would be a sardonic comment on battling for love. This penultimate sequence anticipates the ending of *Venus,* in which the now-dead heroine pleads for a kiss. Oddly, though, it concludes instead with Patty broadcasting from the front, providing a kind of epilogue in which she says that the head's "Be mine" eventually "got rather old," so she would plead with it to say more. But it was unable to speak, for "he had forgotten his hometown lingo" (155). Therefore, she spent twelve years in Paris, coming back "[f]ull of her new words and phrases" (155), and teaching him to speak French. There is a happy ending of sorts, after all:

> And soon they could make decent conversation. They became close. In their way. Made a go of it. Raised uh family. Thuh usual. He told his war stories *en français.* She opened up uh finishing academy and they prospered. And they lived that way. Lived happily ever after and stuff like that. Talking back and forth. This is Ms. Patty. At thuh Front. (156)

Of course, the ending remains bitterly ironic because Patty has been forced to marry a bodiless head, perhaps reflecting the entrapment caused by conventional courtship. Yet a strange glimmer of hope shines in the idea that she teaches her lover to communicate in a new language, suggesting that this is (as opposed to the scripts and rules for love we saw earlier) what makes a marriage work. It's hard not to wonder, though: if it is true that Patty opens up a "finishing academy," will she teach there the fatal precepts that she has discussed with Lily (and would discuss with her own daughter, in the endless cycle of motherhood)? Or will something entirely different be taught?

Choral Explorations of Race and Politics

Imperceptible Mutabilities in the Third Kingdom and *The Death of the Last Black Man in the Whole Entire World*

Imperceptible Mutabilities in the Third Kingdom and *The Death of the Last Black Man in the Whole Entire World* are full-length plays, both of them among Parks's most difficult and enigmatic but rewarding works. With their layered, choral structures and their use of "rep and rev," these two plays carry tremendous power in performance but are challenging to experience on the page. The following discussion will attempt to clarify the works by disassembling the components that make up each; it may be helpful if the reader has the play texts nearby.

Imperceptible Mutabilities in the Third Kingdom

The title of this early play is itself enough to suggest that Parks's works are unlike those of any other dramatist. In 1988, Liz Diamond directed a workshop production of the play at BACA Downtown in Brooklyn; Diamond then directed the world premiere in BACA's 1989 Fringe Festival. The production launched real recognition for Parks in the form of an Obie Award for playwriting; Diamond's direction and Pamela Tyson's performance also won Obies. "Greeks," the last part of the play, was also performed as a separate production (again directed by Diamond) at Manhattan Theater Club's Downtown/Uptown Festival in 1991.

The play has three main parts, with a poetic "choral" section called "Third Kingdom" interspersed. In part 1, "Snails," three black female roommates are being scrutinized by an exterminator-naturalist figure. After the "Third Kingdom" chorus in part 2, we see part 3, "Open House," about an African-American woman named Aretha Saxon, caretaker of two young children, who is literally or figuratively about to "expire." Following a variation of the chorus, the last section, "Greeks (or The Slugs)," is about the Smiths, a military family in which the father is about to return home.

Parks has written definitions of each part of the play's title: the imperceptible is "that which by its nature cannot be perceived or discerned by the mind of the senses"; mutabilities are "things disposed to change"; and the third kingdom is "that of fungi. Small, overlooked, out of sight, of lesser consequences. All of that. And also: the space between" (qtd. in Ben-Zvi 193). Parks's definitions, especially the last, botanical one, are, of course, somewhat tongue in cheek; as we shall see, the resonances of the text are more complicated and allusive than the definitions.

Imperceptible Mutabilities contains early forms of many of Parks's signature elements: choral figures, rep and rev, and inventive phonetic language. More than any other early work, it resembles *Death of the Last Black Man in the Whole Entire World* in its focus on slavery and the history of black experience, as well as in its style and choral structure. Alisa Solomon describes its "allegorical absurdism" as the source of the play's power ("Remarks on Parks 1," 13). S. E. Wilmer points out that it conflates characters and history: "The Naturalist veers from anthropologist to continental conqueror and from pest eradicator to human exterminator. Aretha's tooth extraction becomes confused with the final solution in the concentration camps" (444). At the same time, the play contains autobiographical notes as well as the emphasis on memory that becomes so crucial to her later pieces.

As in *Betting on the Dust Commander* and other works, Parks begins part 1 of the play ("Snails") with a slide show that the actors talk over. Indeed, Parks has called the opening "African American history in the shadow of the photographic image" (Solomon 76). She is deeply interested in the photographic medium and its capacity to lie or tell the truth; often the information in the slide photos competes with or contradicts what the characters say. Parks has commented, "You have these fixed pictures projected up there and down below there's a little person mutating like hell on stage. I'm obsessed with the gap between those two things . . . [as paralleling the relationships between] preconceived images of African-Americans and real people" (qtd. in Solomon 75). Steven Drukman extends the parallel to include critical reactions to Parks's work: "[T]he photograph fixes, freezes, fetishizes, and makes representation static—kind of like what critics do to [Parks]" (66).

Indeed, at the beginning of part 3 ("Open House"), in the second slide show of the play, the characters smile as they would in photographs; Aretha urges her young charges, Anglor and Blanca (names that parodically appropriate whiteness) to smile bigger and bigger for their photos, lamenting that she no longer has teeth of her own. The false smile, the lying smile, invokes Paul Laurence Dunbar's famous poem "We Wear the Mask"; teeth, as we hear later, are "verifying evidence" (53) and are used, for example, to identify a corpse—but Aretha's teeth have been "extracted" as she loses track of her own sense of history. A photograph is a chronicle, but it may be a false one. By the same token, the opening slide show of Molly and Charlene in part 1 reveals a gap between what we are told are "images" of them (Parks leaves to the director the choice of images), and their conversation about Molly leaving school and considering suicide.

Again anticipating the language issues we see in *Last Black Man* (the Prunes and Prisms character), Molly says that she has been expelled from school after being told, "Talk right or youre outta here!" (26). For example, she was given a lesson on the pronunciation of "ask"—"'S- K' is /sk/ as in 'ask'" (25), which suppresses the ebonic "axe." She discusses "lie" versus "lay" and says that she has been ousted from her job: "He booted me. Couldnt see thuh sense uh words workin like he said couldnt see thuh sense uh workin where words workin like that was workin would drop my phone voice would let things slip they tell me get Basic Skills call me breaking protocol hhhhh!" (26). Solomon points out that "the impact of language on self-definition is so crucial here . . . in this first scene the effects of language on self-formulation and social possibility are most explicit" ("Remarks on Parks 1," 12–13). One wonders whether Parks is referring to her own experience of being given a protocol, perhaps in the phone sex job that she fictionalizes so memorably in the screenplay for *Girl 6*.

"Snails" (part 1) sets up one of the play's central themes, the ways in which black culture is misunderstood, misappropriated, or marginalized. This theme is confirmed in the second scene of part 1 when we hear a Naturalist at a podium—possibly a precursor of the Baron Docteur character in *Venus*—describing Molly and Charlene as subjects of scrutiny. This also implicates a playwright, who sets up her characters as subjects for such scrutiny: the audience becomes the "fly on the wall" (27) to which the Naturalist refers. (Solomon also wonders whether Parks is referencing the "white critical establishment" that seeks to describe her work ["Remarks on Parks 1," 14].) But Parks forces us to question the assumptions we make based on sight. As W. B. Worthen puts it, "Parks ridicules 'naturalism'—theatrical and otherwise . . . and alerts the audience to the dynamics of power engrained in relations of visibility: the 'objective' naturalist, the theatrical spectator, and the society that sustains them" (7). Solomon links this problematic scrutiny to the differences between the language that the Naturalist uses and the language that Molly and Charlene use: "Parks shows how egregiously he is missing what's going on in the apartment, in large measure because his language simply cannot describe or encompass it" ("Remarks on Parks 1," 14). Indeed, in the following scene Molly and Charlene talk about a man who goes by "Mokus," of whom there were ninety-nine different pictures at the police station, though "None of um looked like he looked" (28). They link this incongruity to another, an exterminator who "Knew us by names that whuduhnt ours. Could point us out from pictures that whuduhnt us" (28). The connection to the history of false accusations and lynchings of blacks in America is an obvious and powerful one, reinforced by the Naturalist's speech about coming to "teach, enlighten, and tame" in the wilderness (29).

When Dr. Lutzky, the exterminator, arrives in the apartment of Chona, Mona, and Verona, he brags about his prowess and asks to be called "Wipe-em-out" (32) (much as Booth in *Topdog/Underdog* insists that his name is 3-Card, in honor of his future success at three-card monte). James Frieze, in a useful discussion of the play, comments,

> Lutzky, like The Naturalist, does not destroy, but contains by pronouncing that he *can* destroy. Mona and Chona are impressed, not by what Lutzky does (the roaches only grow bigger), but by what his weapons can do. The remote promise of violence serves Lutzky/The Naturalist as an ingenious alternative to actual violence. (526)

Mona, practicing her diction exercises, tells him, "I'm Lucky" (33), a pronouncement echoed later in the choral section by Kin-Seer (39). The characters keep renaming themselves, or go by alternate names (such as Chona/Charlene). In this play, as in *Last Black Man* and other works, Parks is interested in the erasure of names under the legacy of slavery, and in the connections between invention and identity. Her characters often make themselves up as they go along—or attempt to do so.

The tropes of naturalists in the wilderness and of naming/identifying come together in Verona's monologue, which closes part 1 of the play. In the previous scene, we saw her watching *The Wild Kingdom* on TV, and here she professes her love of the show and its host, Marlin Perkins, whose picture she keeps by her bedside at night. Despite her claim that "Marlin loved and respected all the wild things," the evidence reinforces the opposite notion: "His guides took his English and turned it into the local lingo so that he could converse with the natives. Marlin even petted a rhino once. He tagged the animals and put them into zoos for their own protection" (36). This again anticipates—as with the Naturalist—an exploitative fascination with Otherness that Parks later depicts in *Venus.* Even more telling is Verona's story about the black dog her parents gave her: she named the dog Namib "after thuh African sands," but it "refused tuh be trained" and "wouldn't listen tuh me like Marlins helpers listened tuh him" (36). When no one was looking, she would kick Namib, and one day he ran away. In her current job as a "euthanasia specialist" at the veterinary hospital, she says, when someone brought in a similar dog that also "scream[ed] and whine[d] and . . . talk[ed] about me behind my back" (36), she got her apparent revenge as she "Wiped her out!" (37), only to find that the dog looked just like any other dog when she cut it open to "see the heart of such a disagreeable domesticated thing" (37). While it's not clear that Verona (who, in the BACA production, was wearing an African pride T-shirt [Solomon 77]) learned very much from this experience, her anecdote suggests that from an early age we are educated to take for granted certain ideas about imperialism, the taming of the wild, and the need to domesticate "black dogs." Verona's actions, like the many dissections and dismemberments in Parks's works, show the desperation and difficulty of re-membering or understanding how these cycles of exploitation are perpetuated.

Part 2, the "Third Kingdom," which is reprised in different form (i.e., rep and rev) after part 3, is a formal chorus In the original production of the play, Parks replaced what was at first an additional part with a poem, "Third Kingdom," which was split into sections and used as what Diamond calls a "thematic environment" around the other portions of the play ("Remarks on Parks 2," 5); in her 1989 production, the voices in this section were on tape, accompanied by slides of fragmented bodies (Frieze 528). As in *Last Black Man*, the figures in this section announce their names: Kin-Seer, Us-Seer, Shark-Seer, Soul-Seer, and Over-Seer. These names play upon the idea of the choral figures as those who *see*—perhaps as in Greek tragedy—and can see into the future (that is, seers). Yet there is a harsh incongruity between the first four seers and the Over-Seer, whose name evokes the dreaded driver of slave labor on a plantation. Frieze suggests, "Us-Seer seems to embody the home body, standing in both for those who are left behind when slaves depart and those, within the diaspora, who are themselves left behind by practices that divide to conquer" (527). The choral passages speak to the efforts to find identity; Kin-Seer offers a dream of a world split in two, in which (s)he could "see my uther me" waving from the opposite cliff—"but my uther me could not see me" (38). Instead, this other self "was waving at uh black black speck in thuh middle of thuh sea where years uhgoh from uh boat I had been—UUH!" "Jettisoned?" the other figures supply, and Kin-Seer agrees (38). Shark-Seer adds a dream of a fish that swallows him or her and of becoming a shark that washes ashore, is given shoes, and creates a new self: "My new Self was uh third Self made by thuh space in between. And my new Self wonders: Am I happy?" (39).

Just as there is a third self, there is a Third Kingdom, described by Over-Seer as the space of the sea between the two worlds that were created by splitting. Shark-Seer characterizes this space, saying, "Black folks with no clothes. Then all thuh black folks clothed in smilin. In between thuh folks is uh distance thats uh wet space. 2 worlds. Third Kingdom" (39). No wonder that the choral figures keep asking themselves whether they are happy. The Third Kingdom is the Middle Passage, the space between the motherland from which the slaves were brought, and the land of slavery in which they are forced to smile. But it is not just the in-between space of the sea: the Third Kingdom is the space that contains the two worlds and the chasm between them. It is difficult for one world to see across to the other, for the inhabitants of the slave world to recognize their ancestors, or vice versa. As Shawn-Marie Garrett points out, the "figures in [the] Middle Passage keep waving goodbye to their African selves and the distant African shore" ("Remarks on Parks 1," 8). In the reprise of the Third Kingdom chorus, the figures describe trying to wave across, and they make a throat sound characteristic of Parks's speakers, sounds that simultaneously evoke African dialect (the world on one side of the cliff) and being choked or strangled or lynched and thus silenced, suffocated (the world on the other side of the cliff): "Gaw gaw gaw gaw ee-uh. Gaw gaw gaw gaw ee-uh" (56). Their words also comprise a language of the Third Kingdom, a language not easily deciphered by their oppressors: "This is uh speech in uh language of codes. Secret signs and secret symbols" (56).

The images of the forced smile and of slavery are reiterated in part

3, "Open House," which is set simultaneously on the eve of the emancipation of the slaves and in a kind of floating, changeable time period. It includes the aforementioned slide show in which Anglor and Blanca (played in the BACA production by black actors in white-face [Solomon 74]) are urged to have bigger and bigger smiles as they play with their boy doll and girl doll. Aretha, their caretaker (who is about to be released from her duties, her "expiration" literalized in the BACA production by placing her on a hospital bed [Solomon 74]), muses on the number of people she can hold in the house, echoed in the footnotes that Miss Faith gives us about the human cargo capacity of the *Brookes*, a slave ship. The images are linked as Miss Faith goes on to insist that Aretha is due for a (dental) extraction: "You are not cheating me out of valuable square inches, Mrs. Saxon, of course you are not" (44). Worthen remarks, "Miss Faith's well-documented footnotes introduce the public history of the slave trade into the per formed image of its personal consequences, as Aretha is uprooted inside and out" (8). Aretha responds by quoting a biblical-sounding passage in which the Lord is asked for proof that there is a space available within his kingdom, to which the Lord responds with "a toothsome smile" (44). Teeth, of course, are a sure marker of iden-tity, used to identify corpses in cases of doubt. To extract Aretha's teeth is to remove her identity, to separate her from the past, just as slaves were forced to surrender their names and families. As Wilmer says, Aretha "lives through a nightmare of waning identity, changing her name, migrating, losing her teeth and her apartment" (445). Indeed, Charles says to her a few scenes later, "You let them take out the teeth you're giving up the last of the verifying evidence. All'll be obliterated . . . We won't be able to tell you apart from the others. We won't even know your name . . . People will twist around the facts to suit the truth" (53).

In the following scene, the father, Charles, appears; although we are told that it takes place in "Dreamtime" (44), it is punctuated by such details as "Thuh R-S-stroke-26," which Aretha produces when Charles asks for her papers and which Parks explains in a footnote as a "common form from the Division of Housing and Community Renewal" (45). When Aretha says that her husband is dead, Charles tells her to move on because a line has already formed behind her: "The book says you expire. No option to renew" (45). The language thus conflates imagery of slavery (Charles asks whether Aretha and her husband were legally wed or "jump[ed] the broom" [the African/slave marriage ritual]), with imagery of the welfare state (the housing form), a topic to which Parks will return with the characterization of Hester as a welfare mother in *In the Blood*. Indeed, Miss Faith anticipates the later play's character Welfare. Frieze comments, "Just as The Naturalist makes science his posture, a disguise in which he believes, religion gives Miss Faith an excuse for her actions" (528).

Although we are never told what "the book" is, Miss Faith tells Aretha, as she is about to extract Aretha's teeth with pliers, that "[t]he old is yankethed out and the new riseth up in its place" and that Aretha should "[t]hink of it as getting yourself chronicled" (46). Jeanette Malkin notes that "[t]hese extractions are experienced by Aretha as a series of discontinuous moments from her life, plucked out of her through her teeth," and argues that even though the "book" sounds biblical, it is more like "the white history of black America, a chattel listing" (165). Miss Faith adds that the book says Aretha expires "19–6–65" and that the date of June 19, 1865, or Juneteenth, was when the slaves in Texas—"a good many months after the Emancipation Proclamation . . . heard they were free" (47). Aretha's life seems to have been scripted by the book (just as her character's life is dictated by the script of the play itself). Strikingly, though, by scene F of this sequence, the book has also morphed into something more contemporary; namely, Blanca refers to it as the "red herring," which Parks explains in a footnote is "a preliminary booklet explaining the specifics of sale" for a co-op apartment (49). Ownership of human property (slavery) is thus linked to ownership of real estate with all of the rules (and forms of discrimination) there inherent. As they discuss their remodeling plans, though, Anglor and Blanca take things too far ("That iduhnt in thuh book," says Aretha [50]) by proclaiming that as well as being twins, they are lovers. Anglor says, "I would be master. Blanca mistress. That's little master and little missy" (51).

Aretha combines the past of slavery with the past of the Holocaust, as she refers to Buchenwald; Parks points out (again in a footnote) that six million were killed in the concentration camps while nine million Africans were taken into slavery. Aretha seems to disappear into history and into the memory-space of "dreamtime" as Miss Faith tells her that she is free to go. Her insistence that she is making a "histrionical amendment" (53), which injects emotion into history, suggests her efforts not to be forgotten; she is "goin tuh take my place aside thuh most high" (53). This section closes with her insistence that the children smile so that she can photograph them for her scrapbook. Even if they are really crying, she can reshape the memory for herself: "You say its uh cry I say it uh smile. These photographics is for my scrapbook. Scraps uh graphy for my book. Smile or no smile mm gonna remember you. Mm gonna remember you grinnin" (54).

In "Greeks (or The Slugs)," the final part of the play (which appears after another version of the chorus), the Saxon family has been replaced by another family, the Smiths. Again the children have rhyming names (Buffy, Muffy, and Duffy). Solomon characterizes this part as dramatizing the "tragic disintegration of the Smith family" ("Remarks on Parks 1," 13). Parks draws upon her own childhood as the daughter in a military family, for the father is Mr. Sergeant Smith. Hilton Als points out her father sent home audiotapes from Vietnam that may have influenced Sergeant's speeches. Als also suggests that Parks identifies with Muffy, the middle child, in her "refusal to be ignored, to be victimized" (77).

Liz Diamond remarks, "I knew there was something about the stately rhythm of the sound of the text in Greeks . . . that made it seem that there needed to be a very strong choric quality to the family, and that the family somehow needed to have a military bearing. That was something that came from the rhythm of the way they spoke to each other" (Drukman 70). Sergeant Smith opens the part with a monologue that combines meanings of "shots": whiskey, camera shots, and gun shots. As he brags that he is going to be getting his Distinction that day—"Gonna be shakin hands with thuh Commander" (Drukman 58)—his bravado about getting "bars" and sitting behind a desk mutates into the "duck and cover" drills children practiced during the Cold War:

> Because when there is danger from above, we stop. We look. We listen. Then we—dive underneath our desk (being careful that we do not catch our heads on the desk lip). Dive! Dive under our desks where it is safe. Like turtles. In our shells we wait for the danger to pass. (58)

The image of diving picks up on the water/fishing motif that was just represented in the chorus, wherein the seers speak of the water between kingdoms. The confusion represents a childlike point of view wherein the world is not safe but there are protective formulas. As we find out later, Sergeant Smith has been commanded to stay on an island and to keep his rock clean; he speaks of his hope of earning the Distinction, but we get the impression that he has been relegated to janitorial duties. However, by scene E, he claims to have earned it by having "saved uh life" (66).

This picture of the effort to maintain a 1950s-style family continues in scene B, a "lovely home" (60), in which Mrs. Sergeant Smith confers with her daughter Buffy about what the Biloxie Twins are going to wear. Mrs. Smith says that they are going to meet their Maker, a term traditionally used to refer to meeting God after death, but which here seems to mean Buffy's father. The mother reminisces about meeting Mr. Smith on a furlough—as they sat in the rear of the bus. The perfect wife, she is proud of emerging from the journey having "not sweated a drop!" (60). The family has no real idea of what Sergeant Smith's job entails, waiting eagerly for his Distinction that always seems to be in the future. Mrs. Smith repeats, in scene D, variations on her stories about not sweating and about the men from the Effort (i.e., the homeland support for the military) taking the floor lamp; here, the rep and rev technique suggests the monotony of waiting for the military family. Buffy, the first daughter, speaks about the "Censors" as if they, too, were a family. She re-evokes the "language of codes" from earlier in the play, saying that their father "deals in a language of codes—secret signs and signals. Certain ways with words that are plain to us could, for Sergeant Smith, spell the ways of betrayal" (64). Dismembering is invoked as Mrs. Smith remarks that Muffy's name sounds like a minefield, and Muffy responds that a mine is "a thing that dismembers" (64). As elsewhere in Parks's drama, dismembering and losing memory or not remembering (here, the children's fear that their father will have forgotten them) are inextricably linked.

By scene F, the third child—Duffy, the boy—has joined Mrs. Smith and the two daughters as they prepare for Sergeant Smith's arrival home. In Diamond's production, a white actor was cast as Duffy. Parks liked the decision because Duffy represented the "dream child" that the parents hoped not to have to protect ("Remarks on Parks 2," 5). As the characters discuss the differences between humans and other creatures (Sergeant Smith compared himself to a turtle), the sounds and repetitions becoming increasingly choral, increasingly in the style of what later becomes Parks's trademark rep and rev in such plays as *Last Black Man*. This also evokes the image of the Greek chorus, in the title of this part of the play. We see how the previous tropes of the animal kingdom and of evolution come together, as Mrs. Smith says, "Overlap's up gap. Uh gap overlappin. Thuh missin link. Find thuh link" (67). Their choral repetition mutates into a military "Sound off" (68) and Mrs. Smith describes the vision that she had, one that turns out to have a curious resemblance to what happened to Sergeant Smith:

> There was uh light in thuh sky last night . . . Through thuh gap . . .
> Uh man was fallin fallin aflame. Fallin at midnight . . . I heard but
> couldn't do nothin . . . It all happened before you was born. (68)

Sergeant Smith arrives, only to express his disappointment that he was not informed that Mrs. Smith has lost her eyes: "Why haven't we ordered replacements? I woulda liked tuh hear about that" (69). Solomon comments that her blindness is "presumably from trying so hard to see her family as part of the culture that has actually destroyed them" (78). While Duffy, the son, claims that he is the "spittin image" of his father (69), Mrs. Smith insists that there are a lot of Smiths and that she needs documentation of the Sergeant's identity. Parks here literalizes the family's refusal to see or recognize one another. Calling forth the earlier motif of the identification papers and highlighting the common name Smith together reinforce the erasure of identity under racism and slavery (including the folding of slaves' names into their owners').

As he tries to show off his Distinction, Sergeant Smith explains that he finally received it because—in a reflection of Mrs. Smith's vision—he "[c]aught uh man as he was fallin out thuh sky!" (70). But Muffy interrupts his story to say that she read in the paper that he "stepped on a mine" and blew his legs off (70). Again, as in *Last Black Man*, Parks combines mines with memory/dis-membering ("A mine is a thing that remembers," Muffy says [70]) and with possession (Sergeant Smith asks, "You one uh mines?" [70]). Frieze sees his behavior as "a minor but triumphant act of signifying," arguing that "[h]aving been dis-membered in losing his legs, he begins to re-member himself by imposing his way of knowing" (530). Mrs. Smith, who fails to re-member her husband, fantasizes that, when the father gets home, they could have another boy: "Always thought things should come in fours. Fours. Fours. All fours" (70).

In his monologue that closes the play, Sergeant Smith's account of catching the man (now boy) who fell out of the sky becomes, this time, an Icarus myth:

> I saw that boy fallin out thuh sky. On fire. Thought he was uh star. Uh star that died years uhgo but was givin us light through thuh flap. Made uh wish. Opened up my arms—was wishin for my whole family. He fell on me. They say he was flyin too close to thuh sun. They say I caught him but he fell. On me. They gived me uh Distinction. (71)

The Icarus figure falls through the gap between the past and the present—the "flap" to which the Sergeant refers—as if to mark that point of overreaching and the effort to evolve. But the play closes with Sergeant Smith's rueful comment that they aren't even turtles: "We're slugs. Slugs. Slugs" (71). While turtles have shells for homes, slugs—as Wilmer underscores—have no shells and are therefore "homeless" (444). A slug is not only a wormlike creature near the bottom of the evolutionary ladder, but also a bullet or counterfeit coin. As the sounds of an airplane—"evolved" mankind's ability to grow wings and fly close to the sun, as Icarus failed to do—rise up to end the play, Parks presents us with a powerful closing paradox. Humanity strives for ascendance, yet through oppressive social practices such as slavery and war we may fail to recognize our own and others' humanity.

The Death of the Last Black Man in the Whole Entire World

The Death of the Last Black Man in the Whole Entire World is an enigmatic, beautiful, and deeply political play. Parks has said that her idea for it started when she envisioned "the words [of the title] on the wall, the writing on the wall" (Jiggetts 315). She began composing it in 1989, and it was first presented in a staged reading as part of New York Theatre Workshop's "Mondays at Three" Reading Series at the Perry Street Theatre in the 1989–90 season. It was then produced in September 1990 at BACA Downtown in Brooklyn; both the staged reading and the full production were directed by Beth A. Schachter. In 1992, Liz Diamond directed a new production of the play at Yale Repertory Theater. More than in any of her other early works, Parks draws upon figures and tableaux, as well as rep and rev, to create a disturbing (yet at times mordantly comic) view of the situation of the black man in America. Although this work does not have a traditional plot, it centers on the Black Man with Watermelon, who dies repeatedly in the play. In the process, we learn about the forces of history that have brought him to this point. Parks has said the following about the play:

> In Last Black Man, heroism is being there and seeing it through. I guess I have a greater understanding of the small gesture, or the great act that is also very small—like being present. He [the Black Man with Watermelon] is present and trying to figure out what's wrong with him; she's present [Parks is referring to the Black Woman with Fried Drumstick] and trying to figure out what's wrong with him and

what's wrong with her; and the spirit people come to visit and their presence is helpful. ("Women of Color Women of Words")

Parks indicates that the piece is set in the present, though it also has a sense of floating through history or of juxtaposing multiple historical time frames: one of the Black Woman's refrains shows this, as she announces, "Yesterday today next summer tomorrow just uh moment uhgoh in 1317 dieded thuh last black man in thuh whole entire world" (102). Similarly, the Black Man speaks of living in both the past and the present at the same time, though his way of putting it is amusingly confusing: "I bein un uh Now: uh Now bein in uh Then: I bein, in Now in Then, in I will be" (126). As in *Imperceptible Mutabilities*, the narrative mixes biblical lore with folktales, mythology, other literature, and events in black history. And as in that play, choral repetitions (in the chorus passages and in the rep and rev throughout) foreground the musicality of its structure.

The play consists of an Overture, a series of five "Panels" ("Thuh Holy Ghost," "First Chorus," "Thuh Lonesome 3some," "Second Chorus," and "In Thuh Garden of Hoodoo It"), and a Final Chorus. These panel titles are obviously not biblical, but Parks has pointed out that she modeled the structure after the Stations of the Cross, fourteen stations replicating the Passion of Jesus that the faithful can follow themselves. Although there is not an exact correspondence between the fourteen stations and the structure of the play, the parallels are interesting. The Stations of the Cross begin with Jesus being condemned to die, and continue through his carrying the cross, falling three different times, meeting his mother (and later, the Women of Jerusalem), and later dying on the cross and being laid in his tomb ("Stations of the Cross" 1). Similarly, the play follows both the "cross" (condemnation due to his racial identity) that the Black Man is forced to bear, the various figures who assist him during his journey, and his death; the key difference is that the Black Man's "death" is plural and recurring. Liz Diamond describes the play's Catholic connection as follows:

One of the first things we did when we worked on *Black Man* together was to go up to St. John the Divine and St. Patrick's and attend some masses together. She was raised Roman Catholic. So was I. We were both recovering Catholics maybe. Both of us had certain kinds of deep attachments, I must say, visceral attachments to certain aspects of what you might call Catholic ritual . . . I think in her case it was very much connected to rhythm. She was resistant to bringing Baptist rhythms into the piece, particularly at the end. She wanted more the call-and-response of the Catholic church, which is very slow and cadenced. I don't know how to describe it musically, but it's kind of a formal, strict, metric rhythm, as opposed to the more propulsive bending rhythms you might hear in a Baptist church. And that's what we went for. ("Remarks on Parks 2," 13)

The play's lines are also punctuated throughout with the sound of a bell ringing, which may evoke simultaneously a clock's chime, a church bell, a school bell, and a slave's or servant's bell. As in many of avant-garde playwright Richard Foreman's works (Foreman later directed the Public Theater production of *Venus*), the bell has the jarring, Brechtian effect of punctuating the structure, a reminder that we are watching a performance. These forms of acoustic and musical repetition and the visual tableaux create a dramatic piece that mainstream audiences (and students who study the play) may find difficult, but that is highly rewarding in its overall effect.

The Black Man in the play is condemned to (re)enact his own death, by various means: falling (or being pushed) from a twenty-third-floor window (102), the electric chair (108), hanging (118), and so on. His condition reflects that of the statistically endangered African-American male. As Alice Rayner and Harry J. Elam, Jr. put it, "[T]he death of each black man who is hung, electrocuted, hunted down, or has fallen out of history counts equally as the death of the last black man. The death of *every* black man in the past inhabits the death of each black man in the present in the sense that history is lived as a present" ("Unfinished Business" 451). Yvette Louis argues that "[t]he play's context is the history of racial violence and of the discursive and conceptual associations of the black body with the fragmentation that made 'flesh' its primary narrative" (142). In *We Real Cool: Black Men and Masculinity*, bell hooks eloquently describes the plight of the black man in America:

Sadly, the real truth, which is a taboo to speak, is that this is a culture that does not love black males. . . . Black males in the culture of imperialist white-supremacist capitalist patriarchy are feared but they are not loved. . . . If black males were loved they could hope for more than a life locked down, caged, confined; they could imagine themselves beyond containment. Whether in an actual prison or not, practically every black male in the United States has been forced at some point in his life to hold back the self he wants to express, to repress and contain for fear of being attacked, slaughtered, destroyed. . . . Seen as animals, brutes, natural born rapists, and murderers, black men have had no real dramatic say when it comes to the way they are represented. (xi–xii)

Like the characters in Beckett's *Godot*, the Black Man and the figures that surround him are trapped in a hell of repetition that is both metatheatrical (like an actor in a tragedy who is forced to die over and over every night) and ritualistically or symbolically political. It is worth keeping in mind that in order to die over and over, the Black Man also has to be resurrected (resurrection, of course, is one of Parks's favorite themes), thus evoking the play's Christ imagery. Indeed, the epigraph to the play quotes African-American Beat poet Bob Kaufman's lines, "When I die, / I won't stay / Dead" (101). Parks is unafraid of the morbid humor engendered by her topic; when, for example, the Black Man comes home from "work" (being lynched) and the Black Woman says, "Let me loosen your collar for you" (118), the sequence is both macabre and incredibly moving.

As the introductory chapter in this book discussed, the characters in *Last Black Man* are not psychologically rounded or "realistic"; rather, they are *figures* (some of whom are those Parks refers to as "spirit people") in an iconic, historical, representational sense. Bernard refers to the figures in this play as "'ghosts' who refuse to inhabit the confined bodies of realist characters" (690). Again in Brechtian form, Parks is less interested in making us believe that the actors "are" the characters than she is in making us understand their political significance. It is perhaps easiest to place the figures into groups, though there are some cases in which a figure belongs to more than one group.

First, there are the figures that can be connected, through their

Allison L. Payne and Myers Clark in *The Death of the Last Black Man in the Whole Entire World,* director Rob Melrose. Cutting Ball Theater, San Francisco. Photo by Rob Melrose.

names, with food. As in so many of her other works (see, for example, *Pickling* or *Venus*), Parks is concerned with overeating and undereating, with the complicated relationship of gluttony and denial. Louis remarks that "Parks uses food as a powerful metaphoric tool for restoring what has been ruptured on the physical, social, cultural, and linguistic levels. She maximizes food . . . as a vigorous element in re-membering the black body" (160). Images of food and problematizations of consumption pervade her plays, and in *Last Black Man*, some characters are closely identified with food or named for it: Black Man with Watermelon, Black Woman with Fried Drumstick, Lots of Grease and Lots of Pork, Yes and Greens Black-Eyed Peas Cornbread, Ham. Again, in this choral piece, the speakers are not so much characters as iconic figures in African-American culture, and these names connect the soul with soul food. Some of these figures are challenging to embody on stage. Lots of Grease and Yes and Greens pose particular challenges in this regard. Should they be portrayed as eating the food, or is the actor to be costumed to represent the dish itself—or is there an alternative? In Liz Diamond's production of the play, Yes and Greens was portrayed as "an illiterate slave girl"; Diamond saw it as significant that even though she is the "least enfranchised figure in the play," she is the one who repeats the important "You must write it down . . ." phrase ("Remarks on Parks 2," 6). Because Diamond wanted the costumes to be both "high church drag" and historical, the character "wore the rags and pigtails of the pickaninny to be found in the racist cartoons and caricatures of the slave period but glowed with the gold and the glitter of the Promised Land" (Jacobus 1635). An inspired bit of casting in the May 2006 Cutting Ball Theater production of the play, directed by Rob Melrose, was to depict Yes and Greens as an iconic grandmother–church lady in a rocking chair; her "You must write it down" became increasingly impassioned as the play went on.

Parks asks us to walk on the fine line between icon and stereotype. Black Man with Watermelon dies repeatedly by various means (e.g., lynching), representing the historical and statistical mortality rate of the African-American man, or at least the media hyperbole about black men that for years has led to the "pathologizing of the black family" (Louis 144). Bernard characterizes the Black Man's role effectively when she remarks that he "is at once written out of History, yet placed at the center of his own (postmodern slave) narrative. . . . Parks [s]ignifies on the 'tragic' and sacrificial nature of the black subject in literature. . . . [He] is a revision of the folkster trickster figure—he just keeps on coming back" (688). Correspondingly, the figure says—seemingly of the watermelon, but also of the larger stereotypes that have been assigned to him—"Saint mines. Saint mines. . . Saint mines cause everythin I calls mines got uh print uh me someway on it dont got uh print uh me someway on it so saint mines" (105), and later, "Was we green and stripedy when we first comed out?" (107); being "juiced" from the watermelon is conflated with being given the electric chair (107). What is key here, too, is the punishment or denial instead of nurturing: the Black Woman with Fried Drumstick keeps offering him "hen," but he says he "[a]int hungry" and "[a]int eaten in years," adding, "Last meal I had was my last-mans-meal" (106). (This conflation with the Last Supper, making the Black Man a Christ figure, is also deliberate, given that the structure of the play resembles the Stations of the Cross.)

Later in the play, the Black Woman keeps trying to feed the Black Man, and he initially reiterates that he isn't hungry, but she forces him: "Chew on this" (125). Louis, who sees the power of the Black Woman's voice and nurturing advice as central to the play, points out that her "suggestion that eating something will make it your own corroborates that incorporation is an important part of access to power" (143, 157). The Black Man seems to affirm an identity through the memory of food: "Choice between peas and corns—my feets—. Choice: peas. Choice between peas and greens choice: greens. Choice between greens and potatoes choice: potatoes. Yams. Boiled or mashed choice: mashed. Aaah. Mmm. My likenesses" (125). This last word recalls his questions about the watermelon in the wonderful combination of liking and likeness. Eventually the Black Woman is able to feed him until he is "stuffed" (127), which also implies stuffing him like a turkey: we are left with the question of whether the Black Man has a joyful appetite or whether he is being prepared again for his demise. As Venus will do in Parks's later play, he asks to be "re-member[ed]" (128): literally, to be rebodied or reembodied.

The figure of Ham belongs among the food characters, but also among the mythical- political-historical characters, which include Queen-Then-Pharaoh Hatshepsut, Before Columbus, Old Man River Jordan, and And Bigger and Bigger and Bigger and Bigger. One can imagine the actor portraying Ham as holding a large ham, and it is hard not to recall the character of Hambone in August Wilson's slightly later play *Two Trains Running*, who repeatedly says, "He gonna give me my ham." Bernard points out that Zora Neale Hurston also "signifies" on the biblical Ham in her short play *The First One* (694). In Parks's Overture, all of the characters chant a children's song: "HAM-BONE-HAM-BONE-WHERE-YOU-BEEN-ROUN-THUH-WORL-N-BACK-UH-GAIN" (103), referring to the roundness of the world that we shall see in the Before Columbus character. The "hambone" is a traditional juba brought from Africa to the slave plantations in the South, and involves patting one's body in various places while stomping one's feet (its legacy is visible in hip-hop dance styles). Ham, to some extent, is a "ham actor" who wants his voice to be heard and whose performance is over the top, as will be seen in his virtuoso "geneaology"/vaudeville sequence. But he is also the biblical Ham, and calls forth the story of Noah's third son finding his father naked and drunk (Gen. 9:20–22). When Noah discovered this, he cursed Canaan, the son of Ham, to be a servant of Ham's brothers (Gen. 9:25–27). Ham was perceived as the original ancestor of the Cushites, the Egyptians, and the Canaanites (Gen. 10:6); as Rayner and Elam say, "This story grew into a powerful racial myth and a justification for the African slave-trade" (454). Old Man River Jordan says, "Ham seed his daddy Noah neckked. From that seed, comed Allyall" (122).

Ham's monologue in the middle of the play is its showstopper, a virtuoso bit that uses the humor of vaudeville and minstrelsy to parody biblical "origins" stories of the kind found in Genesis. Ham's "Histree" (with the obvious puns on history, on the tree in the Garden of Eden, and on the tree from which the Black Man is hanged) begins, he tells us, in the middle. The following excerpt shows how his "geneaology" tells a story of both presence and absence:

> You (polite) birthed herself Mister, Miss, Maam and Sir who in his later years with That brought forth Yuh Fathuh. Thuh fact that That was uh mother tuh Yuh Fathuh didnt stop them 2 relations from havin relations. Those strange relations between That thuh mother and Yuh Fathuh thuh son brought forth uh odd lot called Yes Massuh, Yes Missy, Yes Maam n Yes Suh Mistuh Suh which goes tuh show that relations with your relations produces complications. (121)

As Rayner and Elam point out, "The humor of the minstrel stump speech derived significantly [from] the speaker's use and misuse of language" ("Unfinished Business" 459) and the speech shows "both the freedom and oppression of language" as "[i]t relies on the virtuosity of the performing actor" (460). Ham creates the structure of a family tree, but the names he gives (which are not really names at all), while comic, speak of the absence of family histories due to slavery, and of the objectification of the slaves themselves. He adds to this slightly later by offering pseudo-biblical "footnotes" that have numbers but no referents, implying both mathematical exponents as well as the parodied scholarship involved in these (non)genealogies: "given she[8] SOLD whodat[33] pairs w/you[23] (still polite) of which nothinmuch comes nothinmuch" (124). The cries of "SOLD" that punctuate this part serve as reminders of the slavery auction block, the act of cutting of legacies and inheritances or knowledge of family histories.

Queen-then-Pharaoh Hatshepsut comes from ancient Egyptian history and ruled in the eighteenth dynasty (about 1479–1458 B.C.). She apparently was not the only female pharaoh in ancient Egypt (though they were scarce), but is distinguished for having dressed like a male (wearing a false beard and male garments) and for creating an unusual number of monuments ("Hatshepsut"). Hatshepsut had been married to her younger half-brother, who died and left her as regent for Thutmose III, her late husband's son by another wife. However, the story goes that her stepson, who eventually ruled again alone after her death, in jealousy erased most of her monuments (Glueck B27, B30). Parks shows her lamenting this: "I left my mark on all I made. My son erase his mothers mark" (116). The Queen describes herself as a member of royalty passing with her entourage: "An I am Sheba-like she be me am passin on by she with her train. Pullin it behind/he on uh plastic chain. Ooh who! Ooh who! Come along" (113). In the process of her description, though, the image of the royal "train" gets confused with the image of a toy train, as if she, too, has become lost in history. It would be possible to envision the actor playing her as bedecked in Egyptian finery, but with something slightly askew, as if she is also an extra from a Cecil B. DeMille epic.

A good number of the Queen's speeches refer to the Before Columbus character, and the two figures are linked because both refer to alternative versions of history that have been covered over by patriarchal Western culture. Before Columbus's name challenges the traditional credit that Columbus gets for having "discovered" America. There were actually voyages to the New World accomplished on African boats much earlier in history, but narratives of these have been erased by racist accounts that would prefer to give credit to a white European. Before Columbus (who might be costumed in traditional African dress) announces:

> The popular thinking of the day back in them days was that the world was flat. They thought the world was flat. Back then when they thought the world was flat they were afeared and stayed at home. They wanted to go out back then when they thought the world was flat but the water had in it dragons of which meaning these dragons they were afeared back then when they thought the world was flat. They stayed at home. Them thinking the world was flat kept it roun. Them thinking the sun revolved around the earth kept them satellite-like. They figured out the truth and scurried out. Figuring out the truth put them in their place and they scurried out to put us in ours. (103)

More specifically, then, the Queen is linked to Before Columbus because of the suggestion that Africans were rulers and explorers long before Christopher Columbus. As Ivan Van Sertima discusses, African voyages to America before Columbus included the launching of the great ships of Mali in 1310 and the sea expedition of the

Justin Chu Cary, Robert Henry Johnson, and David Westley Skillman in *The Death of the Last Black Man in the Whole Entire World*, director Rob Melrose. Cutting Ball Theater, San Francisco. Photo by Rob Melrose.

Mandingo king in 1311 (40–50, 105; see also Bernal). The Queen's descriptions of Before Columbus connect to the play's commentary on language and hegemonic power (to be discussed with the Prunes and Prisms and the Voice on thuh Tee V characters as well). Her description of the difference between "roun" and "round" here is key to an understanding of the play and to Parks's approach to the politics of language:

> Before Columbus thuh worl usta be *roun* they put uh /d/ on thuh end of roun makin roun*d*. Thusly they set in motion thuh end. Without that /d/ we coulda gone on spinnin forever. Thuh /d/ ended things ended. (102)

To put a *d* on the end of "round," in other words, indicates the administration of white Western pronunciation and rules. Doing so puts an end to the freedom embodied in the more onomatopoetic "roun." Louis writes that "[t]he '/d/' at the end of the word represents the change in worldview and the creation of a discourse that fueled conquest, assigned human groups 'their place,' and made the bottom line the motivation for colonialism and expansionism" (151). Controlling discourse is the first step in exerting repressive political control. Thus the roundness of the world—the idea that it could keep on going and going forever—is, ironically, put to a stop (a kind of flattening out) by the imposition of linguistic rules. This helps us to understand Parks's own alternative language choices as an effort to resist hegemony, to resist the rules that would prevent her ways of thinking from "spinnin" into motion. It is also worth considering the resemblance between Parks's "roun" in light of Gates's eliding the closing "g" from "signifyin(g)": "The bracketed or aurally erased *g*, like the discourse of black English and dialect poetry generally, stands as the trace of black difference in a remarkably sophisticated and fascinating (re)naming ritual graphically in evidence here" (46). This "(re)naming"—which Parks also shows as a process of reversion, in which the original naming is lost—is evident here not only "graphically," but as spoken aloud in performance.

Old Man River Jordan's name combines three images. "Old Man

River" is a song from Jerome Kern and Oscar Hammerstein II's 1927 musical *Show Boat* (made into films in 1929, 1936, and 1951), sung by the character of Joe (an older black man with a deep booming voice), and has become a traditional showcase song for black singers, as if it were indeed a spiritual (the great opera singer Paul Robeson sang the most famous version of it). The actor playing Old Man River Jordan might be costumed in the manner of the *Show Boat* character. The River Jordan, of course, is the biblical river that became the allegorical image for the Ohio River in spirituals sung during the era of slavery about the crossing over to freedom from the South to the North. It runs south from the Sea of Galilee to the Dead Sea, and has several biblical resonances: the Israelites crossed it to get to the Promised Land; Jesus crossed it to be baptized by John; and Elijah crossed it before he ascended to heaven in a chariot of fire. But "Jordan" also calls to mind Michael Jordan, who was in the peak of his stardom at the time of the composition of this play, and who represents a certain kind of virtuoso performer. All of these images come together when Old Man River Jordan speaks, since his speeches— done in "scat" style—display a musical virtuosity that evokes, ono-matopoetically, the sounds of the river itself:

> Dribblin by droppletts. Drop by drop. Last news. News flashes then drops. Thuh last drop was uh all uhlone drop. Singular. Thuh last drop started it off it all. Started off with uh drop. Started off with uh jungle. Started spoutin in his spittle growin leaves off of his mines and thuh vines say drippin doin it. Last news leads tuh thuh first news. He is dead he crosses thuh river. He jumps in thuh puddle have his clothing: ON. On thuh other side thuh mountin yo he dripply wet with soppin. Do drop be dripted? I say "yes." (112)

And Bigger and Bigger and Bigger and Bigger's name refers to Bigger Thomas, the protagonist of Richard Wright's classic novel *Native Son* (1940). In that work, Bigger Thomas is condemned to death after he kills a young white woman in a moment of panic; by the end of the novel, he admits to all of the anger that has built up inside of him. To Parks, he represents literary history's portrayal of the black man as both murderer and martyr. He is, in some ways, a double for the Black Man with Watermelon, at one point sharing the Black Man's request that his straps be taken off so that he can move his hands. As the repetitions in the figure's name suggest, he grows and grows throughout history, becoming larger than life. He says of himself, "Sir name Tom-us and Bigger be my christian name. Rise up out of uh made-up story in grown Bigger and Bigger. Too big for my own name. Nostrils: flarin. Width: thickly. Breath: fire-laden and smellin badly . . . I am grown too big for thuh word thats me" (115–16).

Finally, there are the figures of Prunes and Prisms and Voice on thuh Tee V, who overlap with the mythical-political-historical characters, but who also rightly belong in a category that may be called the language-media figures. Because the history behind Prunes and Prisms may not be immediately recognizable, it is worth a short digression to explore the character. Probably the first literary reference to the phrase comes from Charles Dickens's *Little Dorrit*, part of a series of "p" words that the governess Mrs. General advises her young ladies to repeat in order to give their lips a pretty shape (Shklovsky). The term grew to be associated with diction exercises and eventually even to be a synonym for social pretense. It appears twice in Louisa May Alcott's immensely popular works: in *Eight Cousins*, the character of Uncle Alec says, "I take the liberty of differing from Madame Prunes and Prisms, and as your physician, I *order* you to run. Off with you!" And in chapter 21 of her classic *Little Women*, Jo says to Laurie, "Hold your tongue! . . . 'Prunes and prisms' are my doom, and I may as well make up my mind to it" (228). In *A Little Bush Maid* (1910), Mary Grant Bruce has a character say, "She will come out from my mill ground into the most approved type of young lady—accomplishments, prunes and prisms personified!" In 1925 Kansas City journalist Clara Virginia Townsend wrote a book called *Prunes and Prisms, by Percival Prim, The Perfect Speaker*, and she also wrote a regular "Prunes and Prisms" newspaper column.

Of all of these sources, though, the one that seems most directly to have influenced Parks is James Joyce's *Ulysses*, chapter 13: "And the dark one with the mop head and the nigger mouth. I knew she could whistle. Mouth made for that. Like Molly . . . Say prunes and prisms forty times each morning, cure for fat lips." Parks's context for the image is to make it part of learned self- directed racism, and her figure's words paraphrase Joyce's: "Say 'prunes and prisms' 40 times each day and youll cure your big lips. Prunes and prisms prunes and prisms prunes and prisms: 19" (113). This echoes the aptly named character of Molly at the beginning of *Imperceptible Mutabilities,* who is told to practice words like "ask" in order to "correct" her pronunciation. It also calls to mind other characters throughout African-American literature such as Nel in Toni Morrison's novel *Sula,* who is told by her mother to practice such rituals as pulling her nose and wearing a clothespin on it in order to reshape it; Helene, Nel's mother, says, "Don't you want a nice nose when you grow up?" (*Sula* 55). A director might have Prunes and Prisms dressed as a governess or schoolgirl. With this figure Parks calls attention to the his tory of black self- effacement through the use of hair straighteners, lightening creams, diction exercises, and so forth. As an ongoing issue with a long history, such acts are reinforced by media portrayals of "desirable" (i.e., Caucasian) characteristics. Having Prunes and Prisms portrayed by a female would also address the genderized perpetuation of racist self-images. In the context of James Joyce (see the discussion in the introductory chapter), it is also worth mentioning that Joyce's *Finnegans Wake* was based on an old Irish vaudeville tune in which the central character passes out when he is drunk and awakens in the middle of his own funeral, which thus also has interesting resonances for the connection to Parks's play.

Voice on thuh Tee V, probably costumed as an anchorperson (the Cutting Ball Theater cast him as an announcer from the early days of television), represents the media portrayals of black men, reducing them to stereotypes. The Voice gives us a version of the story:

> Headlining tonight: the news: is Gamble Major, the absolutely last living Negro man in the whole entire known world—is dead. Major, Gamble, born a slave, taught himself the rudiments of education to become a spearhead in the Civil Rights Movement. He was 38 years old. News of Majors death sparked controlled displays of jubilation in all corners of the world. (110)

Of course, it would be impossible for all of these "facts" (born a slave, part of civil rights movement, was thirty-eight years old) to be true. Again, various historical times are conflated and confused; Rayner and Elam point out that both Martin Luther King Jr. and Malcolm X were assassinated at the age of thirty-nine (452). Moreover, the idea of the news reporting that the Black Man's death provoked "jubilation" shows the bias against him. Indeed, later, the Voice asks repeatedly, "Whose fault is it?" (123), implying that the media see the black man as at fault in his own death(s). We are told that the Black Man has been keeping his head under the television (102) and that it doesn't fit properly (111); it is as if his head, his identity itself, has been (mis)shaped by the media. While the Voice is part of the play's chorus, then, the figure (like Prunes and Prisms) becomes part of Parks's critique of dominant language and media as they disempower black identity. By the same token, the execution of the Black Man is at one point figured as a spectacle that "[f]olks come tuh watch with picnic baskets" (107), reminiscent of the O. J. Simpson trial; Michel Foucault reminds us of the voyeuristic aspects of early executions that he discusses in *Discipline and Punish*.

For all of these figures, to be part of a history that exists in the dominant culture, among "them" (the "discovery" of America, the visual iconography of African-Americans, etc.) and in other ways to be part of the repressed culture, or "us" (Ham's subversive geneaology, the unerasure of the Queen-Pharaoah, etc.) is to challenge *how* history gets recorded and received. In this sense, the words of Yes and Greens Black-Eyed Peas Cornbread, repeated in various forms throughout the play, evoke the ways that alternative African-American histories have been suppressed:

> You should write it down because if you dont write it down then they will come along and tell the future that we did not exist. You should write it down and you should hide it under a rock. You should write down the past and you should write down the present and in what in the future you should write it down. It will be of us but you should mention them from time to time so that in the future when they come along and know that they exist. You should hide it all under a

rock so that in the future when they come along they will say that the rock did not exist. (104)

Parks implies that history has to be recorded in some way in order to find acceptance. As Bernard puts it, she recognizes "the urgency of History and the need to reclaim experiences and traditions" (691). Much of African and African-American history has been erased from narratives of the dominant culture on the claim that there is no "documentation" for it; the story of Queen- then-Pharaoh represents history that is under erasure because it has the potential to subvert those in power. Subversive or revisionary versions of history, if recorded, sometimes are hidden because they prove threatening. To create such alternative versions means taking on the dominant culture and telling about it from the perspective of the oppressed. However, the possibility remains that the oppressors will claim that the "rock" —that is, the means of preserving the information—was not valid. Thus, Yes and Greens's speech is cynical, but it is also a warning about the need to create and defend alternative historical narratives (specifically of black history), as well as the need to be prepared for the denials these narratives will inevitably provoke.

The play ends with another set of "revisions" of the choral lines, and then with all of the figures saying, "Hold it" (131), repeated seven times. (Jeanette Malkin points out that "hold it" repeated aloud seven times starts to sound like "told it": "a declaration that Parks has herself created memory through . . . performance" [174]). The phrase calls attention to the tableau-like nature of the piece: "hold it" can mean an order to stay still and hold the pose for the audience's contemplation (we might recall Diamond's comment that Parks is interested in the stately aspect of Catholic ritual). Marc Robinson remarks, "The lines capture the contradiction between fixity and flux that gives the play such energy" (189). The Cutting Ball Theater production interpreted "Hold it" as a command for the Black Man when he sits in his coffin and the watermelon is placed in his hands one last time. "Hold it" also means an order to stop, to put an end to what they are doing; in a play that in some ways (like

Godot) is condemned to endless repetition, there is also a request to stop destructive versions of history, to wait and think. The play itself is ultimately the final container to "hold" the re-membering of the Black Man. Parks says that "he's dead but he doesn't know where he's supposed to go . . . his last resting place is within the pages of the play—it's a grave" (Parks, "An Evening").

Anatomizing *Venus*

I look at you, Venus, and see:
Science. You
in uh pickle
on my library shelf.

   —Chorus Member, *Venus* (8)

I have not forgotten my Khoisan
clicks. My flexible tongue
and healthy mouth bewilder
this man with his rotting teeth.
If he were to let me rise up
from this table, I'd spirit
his knives and cut out his black heart,
seal it with science fluid inside
a bell jar, place it on a low
shelf in a white man's museum
so the whole world could see
it was shriveled and hard,
geometric, deformed, unnatural.

   —Elizabeth Alexander, "The Venus Hottentot"

Parks's play *Venus*, first performed in March 1996 at the Yale Repertory Theater and then at the Joseph Papp Public Theater in New York, is one of her best-known and controversial works—and possibly her most significant one to date. The play presents a surrealistic portrait of the historical Venus Hottentot, a Khoikhoi woman named Saartjie Baartman. In Parks's version, we see the consequences of "Venus's" exploitation, first by a sideshow director named the Mother-Showman and then by the Baron Docteur who claims to love her but ultimately dissects her to advance his medical career.

Brought to Europe from South Africa by the trader Hendrik Ceza Boer in 1810, the real-life Baartman was put on display throughout England in the early nineteenth century because of her supposedly enormous posterior. Other artists have taken an interest in Baartman as colonized subject, among them Barbara Chase-Riboud in the 2003 novel *Hottentot Venus*, Elizabeth Alexander in the 1990 poem "The Venus Hottentot" (the title of the volume in which the poem appears), and Renée Green's 1989 mixed-media sculpture *Sa main charmante*. Baartman is still the subject of anthropologists' and sociologists' discussions, often about ethics and ethnography. Her history is part of a larger history characterized by Londa Schiebinger as "radical misreadings of the human body that scholars have described as scientific racism and scientific sexism" (1). Even the question of the rightful place of Baartman's remains, kept until 1994 at the Musée de l'Homme in Paris, is a controversial one. Baartman was a member of the Khoisan tribe, the first people to inhabit the southern tip of Africa (and labeled "Hottentots" by white settlers). Her remains were returned to South Africa under Nelson Mandela's presidency, but the Khoisan people believe they have a right to claim her as a symbol of suffering under colonialism. Cecil le Fleur, chairman of the National Khoisan Consultative Conference Council, says, "Saartjie Baartman became a symbol of our suffering, and all the misery that she went through was a manifestation of how the Khoisan people were treated during that period and beyond" ("Coming Home" 1). Because so much has been written *about* Baartman but so little remains of her own words or voice, she is still an enigma.

Parks writes that when she first heard about the real-life Saartjie Baartman at a cocktail party, "bells started going off in my head" and she knew that she wanted to make a play about this woman: "She was a woman with a remarkable bottom, a woman with a past, and that got me interested in her" (*Venus* 166). Parks's treatment of

Baartman takes some liberties with the "real" story and has been criticized for this reason. Most notably, Jean Young has argued that Parks effectively revictimizes Baartman by undermining her own voice and by downplaying the harshness of historical events (700, 705). The 2006 DePauw University production, directed by Gigi Fenlon, engendered similar controversy. But it is important to remember that Parks is using Baartman for *theatrical* purposes to create what is also a larger and more allegorical story—and one that is also an apt representation of her unique dramatic style. Harry Elam and Alice Rayner, in their important essay on this topic, provide what is probably the most balanced and convincing response to the allegations about Parks's complicity in exploiting Baartman:

> Both the spectacle and the narrative fail to produce the real Baartman, or the real story. She is built up artificially and rises out of the gaze of her spectators; narratives falsify and fragment her on stage, giving satisfaction only to an audience: between, Parks leaves a space for the real, if absent Baartman. ("Body Parts" 273)

Parks quotes Emily Dickinson's line "Tell all the Truth but tell it slant," adding, "With *Venus* my angle is this: *History, Memory, Dis-Memory, Remembering, Dismembering, Love, Distance, Time, a Show*" (*Venus* 166). Her nonlinear, multilayered narrative and her choral, circuslike construction of the play implicate the audience in a voyeuristic fascination with the anatomy of the Venus Hottentot; they suggest the relationships among the exploitation of Saartjie, the history of colonialism, and contemporary white appropriations of black culture, or what bell hooks calls "eating the Other" (181).

It is striking that, as Londa Schiebinger points out, no record exists of Baartman's original (African) name, only her Dutch one (12). Throughout the play, Parks shows us a negation or misunderstanding of Venus's language; perhaps one response to Jean Young would be that the play reflects the real silencing of Baartman's voice by revealing ways in which it is repeatedly vanquished. Interestingly, the Mother-Showman tries to describe the Hottentot language as "uh whole language of kicks" (46), and her phrase echoes and rhymes with the Baron Docteur's later description:

Amberlin Morse in *Venus*, director Gigi Fenlon. DePauw University Theatre. Photo by Matt Bowen.

> Our Anthropological scholars present will remember that
> although, while during her stay with us, she picked up
> uh bit of English, French, and even Dutch all *patois*,
> the native language of this woman is said
> to have consisted entirely
> of an almost uninterrupted succession
> of clicks and explosives.
> (*Rest*)
> A language of *clicks*, Gentlemen.
>
> (95)

This reflects what Stephen Greenblatt describes in *Learning to Curse* as the pervasive belief when the New World was discovered that the savages were "without eloquence or even without language," a belief upheld, for example, in Shakespeare's Caliban claiming not to have had language until given it by Prospero (21). When Venus does attempt to speak—as in the scene in which she defends in court her right to be exhibited because "[s]howing my sinful person as a caution to you all could, in the Lords eyes, be a sort of repentance and I could wash off my dark mark" (76)—we realize that she has been co-opted by the beliefs of the white Europeans. We see a conflation of the images of "discovery" when Venus tells the Baron Docteur, "You could be whatsisname: Columbus . . . You could discover me" (104, 108). The Baron Docteur, denying that he had any real relationship with Venus, says, "I am to her a mere Anatomical Columbus" (131). Schiebinger points out colonial relationships "were often portrayed using female figures as in William Blake's depiction of Europe supported by Africa and America" (15). As in *Last Black Man,* Parks underscores the links between the colonizing of the individual and a larger history of colonization and exploitation.

Why the focus on the "black bottom"? Like Toni Morrison, who makes this physical image into a geographic metaphor in *Sula*—and like August Wilson, who uses it in his play *Ma Rainey's Black Bottom* (1979) to foreground the exploitation of a black blues singer—Parks is interested in contemporary reverberations of the historical depiction and appropriation of the "black bottom." In an interview with Una Chaudhuri, Parks comments that "the butt is the past, the posterior; posterity. She's a woman with a past, with a big past—History" ("For Posterior's Sake" 34–35). As Michele Wallace points out, "Visual differentiation was the foundation of most thought about race and sexuality during this period," and these acts of differentiation were reinforced by the rise of the "spectatorial imagination of the West, the gaze, the need to study and examine 'the other'" through newly popularized means such as photography, film, and the freak show (31). Parks evokes this "posterior," this history, but the play's Brechtian style suggests that we cannot put it behind us. Greg Miller points out that more than posteriority is at issue: "*Venus* is dominated by real and hypothesized holes, gaps, absences, and voids" (128). Elam's and Rayner's parsing of Parks's words is a useful one: "Parks's method . . . is to find ways to embody language: here she moves from the body to the word (*posterior*), uses a cognate word (*posterity*) and traces from physical sense to a concept of history" ("Body Parts" 271).

Even the "bottom" of the play—its end—is more or less placed in front of us first (see Miller 134). As one of the its stylistic devices that might be called Brechtian, the play's scenes are numbered in reverse order, beginning with an Overture and counting down from scene 31 to scene 1; the narrator figure, the Negro Resurrectionist, announces the number and title of most scenes at the end of each previous one. Yet the plot of the play does not proceed backward, as in Harold Pinter's *Betrayal*; the Overture announces that "the Venus Hottentot is dead" (3), but we then move forward in time from Venus's original "capture" in Africa to her death in prison after the Baron Docteur has given her back to the authorities. As Elam and Rayner point out, the irony is that despite the Overture's announcement that there will be no show tonight because Venus is dead, "[T[here is certainly a show" ("Body Parts" 268)—one we are watching in complicit spectatorship. The counting down of scenes underscores the inevitability of Venus's demise; moreover, the dividing of the play into short titled scenes has the function, as in Brecht, of reminding us that we are seeing fragments—parts rather than a whole—and that these fragments are overtly theatrical.

As in some of her other works, such as *The America Play*, Parks includes "academic" devices such as footnotes and historical extracts to highlight the textual nature of the piece and the unreliability of texts. In scene 28, for example, the Negro Resurrectionist reads, "Footnote #2: *(Rest)* Historical Extract. Category: Medical. Autopsy report" (28). The insertion of actual newspaper accounts and the like—a device also used in such pieces as Moises Kaufman's *Gross Indecency*, about the trials of Oscar Wilde—forces us to see both the fictionalized dramatic narrative and the "real" historical excerpts as contesting accounts: neither one is completely "true" or completely "false." Through this device the play juxtaposes two layers of narrative time: the historical past (the setting of the play), and the present tense for the audience (reinforced by anachronistic diction ("Uncle took Dad to Africa," says the Young Man. "Showed Dad stuff. Blew Dads mind" [26]).

Some critics responding to the 1996 Public Theater production (directed by Richard Foreman) had a mixed reaction to this Brechtian structure. Michael Feingold, writing in the *Village Voice*, feared that it undercut our sense of Baartman's humanity:

> The story ostensibly progresses, but its beginning and end are always apparent; through the repetitions, every event is visible in every other event. While this is often fascinating to listen to—and to watch, as Richard Foreman's flamboyant staging matches Parks's reconfiguring words with constant visual rearrangements—it keeps a maddeningly rigid distance from the life and times of a woman who was, in the first instance, a human being, and whose humanity is presumably the source of Parks's interest in her. (81)

It is surprising that Feingold —himself an adaptor of Brecht's work— was not more favorably disposed to Brechtian devices that create a wrenching sense of the political forces behind the exploitation, and ultimately, of our complicity with these forces. Michele Wallace's response to the Public's production provides a countertext to Feingold's:

> While the actress Adina Porter does a moving job of endowing Baartman with humanity, the play isn't necessarily about the empirical experience of the actual woman, what it was really like for Saartjie Baartman to be exhibited nude, to be stared at by white men fascinated with her buttocks. More important to Parks, I imagine, is to come to terms with the variables that created the situation. (31)

In addition to footnotes, historical extracts, and the like, Parks creates a recurrent intertext of a mock-period piece called *For the Love of the Venus* (which bears a resemblance to plays such as *The Hottentot Venus or the Hatred of French Women*, staged in Paris in November 1814 [Worthen 11]). In this play-within-the-play (watched with great interest by the Baron Docteur), schematic characters (the Young Man, the Bride-to-Be, etc.) act out a love story wherein the Bride-to-Be, upon advice from her mother, dresses up as the Venus Hottentot in order to reawaken the interest of the Young Man, who has become fascinated with her exoticism at the expense of his ardor for his bride. In Baartman's time black women "served as foils to the Victorian ideal of the passionless woman, becoming . . . the central icon for sexuality in the nineteenth century" (Schiebinger 7–8). In the 2001 Oberlin College production directed by Shannon Forney, the *For the Love of the Venus* sections were performed on a mini-stage and the actors behaved like puppets, underscoring their overde-termined, mechanized nature. The characters recite in a period-appropriate verse style—punctuated by the aforementioned anachro-nisms. This play-within-the-play acts as a historical comment upon the reactions to the Venus at the time (and the desire to make her into "art," thus perhaps also poking fun at Parks's own attempt to do the same). It calls attention to the colonialist impulses behind the exhibition of Venus: like the banana that the Young Man's father brings back from Africa, she becomes a consumable object (an image reinforced elsewhere in the play by the associations of Venus with chocolate). Moreover, we witness the Young Man's longing for "something Wild" (48) that is both indulged and domesticated.

Throughout *Venus*, Parks uses the structure of "rests" and "spells" (discussed in the introduction). She includes an excerpt from her "Elements of Style" at the beginning of the play text to illustrate the textual appearance of her "spells":

The Venus
The Baron Docteur
The Venus
The Baron Docteur (iv)

At one point in the play, this "spell" constitutes an entire "scene of Love" between these two characters; the power of the scene resides in the mutual silence characterized by the deep differences between what, we would imagine, each of the two characters is thinking or feeling. As mentioned in the introductory chapter, Jennifer Johung sees this scene as emblematic of Parks's spells. She notes that "the scene of spells is not merely unspecific, but usefully so," explaining that the silence calls our attention to the "negotiation" between the black body of Venus and the white, European body of the Baron Doc-teur (41). These devices form part of Parks's Brechtian structure, because such moments encourage a critical contemplation of the characters and an awareness of their onstage transactions *as* transac-tions, thematizing commodification and exploitation.

The set design for Foreman's production incorporated his characteristic visual style (which includes "alienating" devices such as strings, intrusive lights, and noisemakers), which also reflected the Brechtian nature of Parks's text. Center stage, at the top of the proscenium arch, a red light blinked throughout the play. The set itself was overhung with a network of strings; as John Lahr describes it, "The spectators peer through Foreman's trademark lattice of plain and patterned strings, which crisscross above them and across the front of the stage like telephone wires, at once forcing an audience to keep its distance and to look harder" (98). Foreman characterized the strings as a reflection of his own childhood interest in the circus (Shewey 5), which is apt for a play caught up in freak shows and circuslike displays. Later productions (such as at Oberlin College) have made greater use of the circus aspect, drawing the audience in as freak-show gawkers, a role that causes them (one hopes) to question their own participation, as shall be discussed shortly.

Possibly the most difficult decision for any production is the costuming of Venus herself. What about the famous rump for which she was exhibited? To what extent is she sexualized? In the Public Theater production, Adina Porter was outfitted with exaggerated body parts, including prosthetic buttocks, so that her appearance was almost cartoonish. Interpretations of this choice have been varied. Rayner and Elam write, "The butt clearly did not belong to the actress, but it nonetheless gave the effect of total exposure" ("Body Parts" 271). Johung comments that this strategy "framed Porter's lack of a huge posterior as present, foregrounding the presence of absence" (49). Rather differently, W. B. Worthen sees the padding as a metaphor for the attempt to stage Baartman in the first place, for the play itself "stages . . . Baartman as prosthesis, stand in, surrogate—as The Venus" (11). When Venus wears a padded costume, then, the audience sees her as her onstage spectators see her—and is forced to be cognizant of the distortions of that vision. Some critics, however, believed this portrayal risked making Venus into an object of ridicule. It is striking that many scholarly discussions of the play assume that Venus must be costumed in padding and prosthetics, though this is certainly not the case.

The Oberlin College production chose the opposite extreme,

making Venus decidedly nondescript by outfitting her in a plain tan dress, marking the contrast between her and the other "anatomical wonders" of the Mother-Showman's act. This portrayal highlighted the mythology of Venus's body as a projection by the characters within the play. The production added a giant Venus puppet, divided into anatomical sections with words like *Science* written on them, which was assembled and disassembled by members of the chorus. This allowed a Brechtian scrutiny of the way in which Venus was broken down into anatomical "parts" and inscribed with the scientific language of her colonizing oppressors. Yet one wonders whether the play's political challenge to the audience was lessened because the puppet distracted us from assessing our status as participants in gazing at Venus's body. It may be crucial to affirm, as Shawn-Marie Garrett writes, that "Venus is the one in the spotlight, being described as subhuman, but the discomfort is felt equally by the spectators, who can't take their eyes off her" (132). It is perhaps with this motive in mind that some productions may choose a third alternative, namely of portraying Venus in a sexually provocative manner (by putting her in a skimpy costume, for example): while this reenacts a certain violation of Venus (or of the actress playing her), it also puts the audience members in the (one hopes) uncomfortable position of voyeur and encourages their self-recognition of their role.

The colonialist attitude that Baartman had "an intensely ugly figure, distorted beyond all European notions of beauty" (36) was at the bottom of her exploitation. It also became, in Parks's representation, her self-image: she learns to see herself as her exploiters see her, as a sexualized object. The Overture features a "revolving" Venus who rotates as the other characters announce her presence; one Chorus Member, addressing the (real) audience as circus freak show spectators, announces that her posterior is "[w]ell worth the admission price. A spectacle a debacle a priceless prize, thuh filthy slut" (7). Venus is aware of the need to perform once she has been forced into her role. When the Mother-Showman tells the spectators, "Observe: I kick her like I kick my dog!" the stage directions indicate that the kicking "has the feel of professional wrestling but also looks real"

Amberlin Morse and others in *Venus*, director Gigi Fenlon. DePauw University Theatre. Photo by Elizabeth Andrews.

(45). These are the boundaries between performance and the "real" that blur throughout the play, in part because Venus participates. She has no choice (she is asked whether she wants to leave Africa, but the choice is a sham, and the Baron Docteur makes her "choose" to have an abortion). Venus is intelligent and gifted, yet each time she asserts these talents, she is suppressed. She tells the Mother-Showman that she can count, but the latter insists her ability should be "our secret" (40); when Venus says, "We should spruce up our act. I could speak for them. Say a little poem or something," the Mother-Showman replies, "Yr a Negro native with a most remarkable spanker. Thats what they pay for . . . Theres the poetry" (51). Later, when the Anatomists are impressed by how quickly she picks up French, the Baron Docteur insists that her abilities are simply "one most glorious exception" to the proofs of the inferiority of her race (112). When she tries to transcend her given roles, Venus is reinserted within the symbolic order.

A production of *Venus* must understand the vital role of the Negro Resurrectionist. Although on the surface he is simply an emcee, the repercussions of his character go much further, both in the play itself and within Parks's work as a whole. Worthen comments that "Parks invents the Negro Resurrectionist not so much to resurrect Baartman, but to resurrect the ways in which she has been dis/re-membered" (16). Rayner and Elam remind us that as "master of ceremonies," the Negro Resurrectionist is "a theatrical entity [and thus] he is complicit in the exploitation" ("Body Parts" 274). As the announcer of each scene, the Negro Resurrectionist is the classic narrator in the tradition of Shakespeare's prologue in *Henry V* or the Stage Manager in Thornton Wilder's *Old Town*. In Brechtian terms, he—along with the unusual sequencing of the narrative—limits the audience's involvement with "plot" and encourages an investigation of the why and how of Venus's exploitation and demise. Unlike in Shakespeare or Wilder, however, the Negro Resurrectionist is himself a crucial character within the plot. Early in the play, after Venus has just finished taking a bath, she catches him watching her and says, "What you looking at?" He replies, "Yr lovely," and a "spell" between them follows (35). Parks comments, "Yes, there's a lot of watching in Venus . . . the doctor is watching Venus, and the Resurrectionist is watching everybody. Then actually at the end he becomes the watch, the death watch on Venus. So, it's all this kind of looking" (Jiggetts 313). To some extent, then, she invites us to see the Negro Resurrectionist and Venus as parallel characters who are both exploited by their dominators. The Negro Resurrectionist has been hired to do the dirty work that the white men won't do. As he explains to Venus,

I used to dig up people
dead ones. You know,
after theyd been buried.
Doctors pay a lot for corpses
but "Resurrection" is illegal

and I was always this close to getting arrested.
This Jail-Watchmans jobs much more carefree.

(158)

When the Negro Resurrectionist is standing guard over the encaged Venus, the Grade-School Chum approaches him and says, "You used to unearth bodies for my postmortem class. An illegal craft as I remember" (150). When the Negro Resurrectionist responds that it has been years since he has done that kind of work, the Grade-School Chum responds, "Once a *digger* always one" (150). He offers gold to the Negro Resurrectionist for providing him with the body of Venus once she dies, kneeing him in the groin and threatening to call the police and have him locked up for his previous illegal activities if he refuses. After a "spell" sequence in which the two regard one another, the Negro Resurrectionist says, "Alright, I guess. I mean, who is she to me?" and the stage directions indicate that "[h]e takes the coin but feels like shit" (152). Thus, a potential ally for Venus is powerless to prevent himself from becoming complicit in her exploitation.

The Grade-School Chum's label of "digger" for him rhymes with the racial slur, but to be a digger/resurrectionist is also part of Parks's iconography, as is obvious in *The America Play* and other works. Digging into history to find what has been buried or lost is, in Parks's dramatic universe, a central task in rewriting the black past. In describing her process in writing *Venus*, Parks tells Una Chaudhuri, "I didn't know anything about her and I had to go to the library and dig and dig and dig" ("For Posterior's Sake" 34). One of the play's repeated choral lines, prompted by the Negro Resurrectionist himself, is "Diggidy-diggidy-diggidy-diggidy" (3). A "resurrectionist" is a charismatic religious figure, like an emcee or a preacher, but he is also one who returns (or returns others) from the dead. One of the quotations used in the stagebill for the Public Theater production was from Susan M. Shultz's *Body Snatching:* "Resurrectioning or resurrectionists, grave robbers, fishermen, snatches, grabs, and sack-em-up men refer to the practice of illegal disinterment of human remains and the persons who perform the work" (28). Both *The*

Amberlin Morse and Teddy Tutson in *Venus*, director Gigi Fenlon.
DePauw University Theatre. Photo by Elizabeth Andrews.

America Play and *Topdog/Underdog* feature black Abraham Lincoln
impersonators who re-create Lincoln's assassination (that is, they die
and are resurrected over and over again); *Last Black Man*, as we have
seen, kills and resurrects its protagonist over and over amid a choral
evocation of America's past sins against black humanity. Here in
Venus, Parks resurrects the real- life historical figure of Baartman.
The Negro Resurrectionist is complicit in stealing her body, but he is
as well the one who goes on to tell her story, thus (as announcer, and
to some degree as an author surrogate who is also not immune to
exploitation) digging up her history.

Like Caryl Churchill *(Cloud Nine)*, Tony Kushner *(Angels in
America)*, and other neo- Brechtian playwrights, Parks experiments
with double-casting and cross-casting to remind us of the Brechtian
sense that "character" is a construction and that the actor and character are not one seamless entity. Parks tells Una Chaudhuri, "I
wanted to give these actors the opportunity to play lots of characters

and change roles a lot. Because it's all about the Show" ("For Posterior's Sake" 35). Choosing the same actor to portray the Baron Docteur and the Man who is interested in Venus in Africa, and a single actor to play the Man (in Africa's) Brother, the Mother-Showman, and the Grade-School Chum sets up a cross-commentary on the ways Venus is exploited as a sexualized object (in the first instance) and as an expendable commodity (in the second instance). Similarly, one set of eight actors plays the Chorus of the 8 Human Wonders, the Chorus of the Spectators, the Chorus of the Court, and the Chorus of the 8 Anatomists. Parks thus creates parallels among these different groups of onlookers who participate in the objectification of Venus and who ultimately are linked to the actual spectators of the play themselves. As Miller points out, she extends the double-casting by often allowing the characters to cross the boundaries of time and space, such as when the Baron Docteur is seen as the audience (and thus also as an onstage replication of us as spectators) to the *For the Love of the Venus* play (130).

As should already be clear, it is vital that a production of *Venus* unsettle its spectators. Garrett remarks that "Parks's audiences . . . travel through her theatre's repetitions and revisions to arrive at an understanding that they, too, must count themselves among history's dupes" (26). One of the most powerful encouragements to the spectators to question their own status as voyeurs is the play's intermission, which is not really an intermission at all, but creates (as in some of Luigi Pirandello's works, e.g., *Tonight We Improvise*) a collision between the "break" during which the audience expects to stretch, use the restroom, have a drink, make a phone call, and the continuation of the play's action. In this case, the house lights come up, but Parks has the Baron Docteur giving a lecture on the anatomical properties of Venus, explaining (in graphic scientific language) the findings of his postmortem research on her body. Several times during this sequence, the Baron Docteur addresses the audience members directly as if they were the medical colleagues in attendance at his lecture, thus implicating them as willing participants in the vivisection of his subject:

I do invite you, Distinguished Gentlemen,
Colleagues and yr Distinguished Guests,
if you need *relief*
please take yourselves uh breather in thuh lobby.
My voice will surely carry beyond these walls and if not
my finds are published. Forthcoming in *The Royal College*
Journal of Anatomy.
Merely as an aside, Gentlemen.
(Rest)

The Baron Docteur creates a conflict for the spectators between the
urge to stay and listen, and the urge to attend to other "intermission"
needs, as he does by reassuring them here and at other points that it
is fine for them to leave because his voice will carry out into the hall-
way. At one point he singles out from the audience a "Distinguished
Colle[a]gue" who looks like he needs "relief or sleep" (95), presumably a real audience member who looks torn between the desire to
stay and the desire to go.

Although Greg Miller argues that Parks is making the audience
"turn its back" upon the details of the postmortem (135), I would
argue that the effect in productions of the play has been rather different. At the Public Theater performance I attended, the audience
members seemed extremely, amusingly uncomfortable at not having
a "real" intermission and (since the production was in a small house)
of having their decision to stay or to leave remarked upon at times by
the Baron Docteur. A slip of paper was placed in the stagebill (possibly in reaction to the audience's confusion?) that read:

PUBLIC NOTICE
Midway in the Intermission
of this performance
of
Venus
by Suzan-Lori Parks,
for those with a Scientific Bent,
the Most Distinguished
BARON DOCTEUR
will lecture on
the various Physical Aspects

of the Venus Hottentot
on the stage of Martinson Hall

Of course, on some level the (deliberate) slippages in this announcement between the worlds of the production (mentioning the author's
name and the name of the actual auditorium) and the world of the play
(the Baron Docteur's lecture) may increase the confusion, but doing so
adds to the Brechtian/Pirandellian refusals to separate these worlds.

The Oberlin College production, on a proscenium stage in a large
auditorium, provoked the audience in a different manner. In this
case, the audience members circulated freely and talked loudly; the
Baron Docteur responded by becoming more and more frenetic in his
lecture in a (rather futile) attempt to regain the audience's attention,
as if he were losing control of his scholarly demeanor. Meanwhile,
the cast members playing the Chorus of the 8 Human Wonders wan-
dered throughout the house distributing chocolates to the spectators,
some of whom vied rowdily with one another to receive them. I will
discuss the chocolates shortly, but suffice it to say that despite
markedly different approaches to the intermission, both productions
brought out the Brechtian challenge to the audience: our self-aware-
ness, our embodiment, as spectators is foregrounded at the same
time that our ability to pull away from the action (or from our complicity with it) is disallowed.

The graphic nature of the Baron Docteur's speech itself also presents a direct challenge to the audience (and the text of the play
includes a glossary of medical terms). One does not ordinarily think
of an autopsy report as "theatrical" material, even though there are
certainly overlaps between medical and theatrical language (the oper-
ating "theater," for example). Careful listeners (and certainly readers)
will understand that part of the "scientific" fascination with Baartman was due to what was seen as her pronounced genitalia. According to Schiebinger, "[N]othing excited these [scientists] more than
the elongation of the labia minora, or inner vaginal lips, among the
Hottentot. This 'Hottentot apron' became the subject of countless
books and articles, and much prurient popular and scientific speculation" (10). Before her death, when Baartman was brought to the

Jardin du Roi to be examined by a team of scientists that included Georges Cuvier (the real-life Baron Docteur), Henri de Blainville, and Geoffroy Saint-Hilaire, she was very reluctant to remove the cloth that covered her genitals and was particularly repelled by de Blainville, who at one point offered her money (Schiebinger 12–13). When Cuvier began his vivisection of Baartman after she died about nine months later, he wrote of this "apron" that "there is nothing more celebrated in natural history" (Schiebinger 11). In his report within Parks's play, the Baron Docteur creates a linguistic equivalent of his vivisection of Venus. One of the controversial questions about the play, then, is whether Parks herself is participating in disrespectful resurrection of Baartman's body by allowing it to be symbolically dismembered again and again in front of an audience via the Baron Docteur's speech. Una Chaudhuri asks Parks directly in her interview, "[Y]ou are remembering someone who was both literally dismembered but also taken apart in terms of her meaning—dispersed among many medical and legal and anthropological and literary texts, excerpts of which are quoted in the play. Was part of your idea to find out what had not been captured in that way?" Parks responds, "Yes, the play itself is that: it's what didn't get used up or chopped up. It bears her name, now it is her body, her resurrection" ("For Posterior's Sake" 35). Hence, the play invokes the merged images of remembering and re-membering (i.e., putting the pieces back together), of dis-re-membering (forgetting, or disrespecting), and dismembering (taking apart). The play itself is therefore an act of re-membering Venus/Baartman, of recollection and of putting the parts back together with a concomitant awareness that it is never possible to do so. This attempt to re-member, then, stands in marked contrast to Cuvier's vivisection report, as played out in the Baron Docteur's speeches and as reported by Schiebinger:

> Cuvier's now notorious memoir described the Hottentot Venus in remarkably unflattering terms. At every turn he found her physique and manner bestial. He compared her protruding buttocks, an "elastic and shivering mass," to the buttocks of mandrills and of other monkeys. . . . She had great pendular breasts and the unsightly habit

of making her lips protrude like an orangutan. Her thigh bones were heavy and short like an animal's. . . . She danced in the manner of her country, and played with a fairly good ear upon a Jew's harp. She liked necklaces, belts of glass beads, and other "savage finery." She drank too much. Though by his own report she was gay, had a good memory, and spoke three languages, Cuvier also remarked that while her hands were charming and feet pretty, her ears were small like those of apes . . . Only one short paragraph evaluated her brain. (13)

Positioning the audience members as consumers is central to Parks's emphasis on Venus's seduction by the image of herself as a consumable object (this insistence, too, became part of the play's controversial critical reception). Part of the Baron Docteur's success with Venus is due to his developing in her an insatiable desire for chocolates (a substitute for the apparent alcoholism of the real Baartman). The chocolate is a replication of Venus's own colonization and thus becomes one of the play's key images of Western culture's desire to appropriate and consume the "Other." In a speech to the audience called "A Brief History of Chocolate" (155–56), Venus relates that chocolate was in the New World a commodity thought to have mystical and aphrodisiacal properties. She alludes to the tradition in which women are presented with chocolates as a profession of love, and mentions its purported ability to calm women in the face of "emotionally upsetting incidents" (156). John Henderson notes that chocolate was thought to have powerful medicinal properties, quoting a document from 1631:

[Chocolate] vehemently incites to Venus, and causeth conception in women, hastens and facilitates their delivery; it is an excellent help to digestion, it cures consumptions, and the cough of the lungs, the New Disease, or plague of the guts, and other fluxes, the green sicknesse, jaundice, and all manner of inflammations and obstructions. It quite takes away the morpheus, cleaneth the teeth, and sweeteneth the breath, provokes urine, cures the [kidney] stone, and expels poison, and preserves from all infectious diseases. (1)

In a monologue, Venus says that her favorites among the chocolates are the "Capezzoli di Venere," the "nipples of Venus" (a glossary of chocolates appears the end of the play text), implying that she has become a participant in her own consumability. Worthen suggests that this monologue is "the most self-evidently 'theatrical' in the play, a moment where The Venus is cited through emphatically fictitious means" (15). In an earlier monologue (scene 7), Venus fantasizes about being introduced to members of high society and attended to by servants; we see the extent to which she has internalized the power dynamic of the server-servant relationship. Her most vivid fantasies involve being waited upon, just as she herself has been made to do the bidding of others:

> Come here quick, slave and attend me!
> Fetch my sweets! Fix my hair!
> Do this do that do this do that!
> Hahahahahahah! Mmmmmmmm.
>
> (136)

The chocolates the Baron Docteur feeds Venus become a drug, a means of placating or distracting her; at one point, when he is about to masturbate in her presence, the Baron Docteur tells Venus, "Dont look! Dont look at me. Look off somewhere. Eat yr chockluts eat em slow thats it. Touch yrself. Good. Good" (106). And again, the audience is complicit in the maintenance of her status. When the spectators of the Oberlin production were thrown chocolates during the intermission, their consumption of Venus as the object of the gaze became more than just visual; their eagerness to "digest" was mocked even as they were being soothed or placated with food. And Greg Miller reminds us that "[t]he trope of chocolate has contemporary relevance as well, considering the rise of child slavery in the cocoa fields of western Africa (especially the Ivory Coast)" (136).

Feeding Venus chocolates not only keeps her subservient, but also instills the sense that if she is to have any agency, it must involve, ironically, maintaining the image of herself as a fetishized object. John Lahr remarks, "In her drive for attention and wealth, she is trapped in a performance from which she cannot extricate herself. She is an object of desire but not of love, an unwitting queen of avoirdupois and alienation" (98). When Adina Porter, playing Venus in

Foreman's production, was asked about Venus's complicity in her own fate, she replied:

> To what extent did the Venus Hottentot . . . have an opportunity to refuse? Her homeland had been vanquished nearly 140 years before her birth, not only by violence and intimidation, but by alien diseases like smallpox. Her race was labeled as "primitive" and legally subjugated as slaves, and her gender was considered "God's gift of comfort in the wilderness." She did not have much experience saying no. Yes, the Venus Hottentot wanted financial independence. Yes, she wanted to be loved—most people still believe that to be the ultimate validation of a woman's worth. Did she willingly allow herself to be treated like a "rare bird"? In her world, it was better than being a beast of burden. The irony is that when a treasured pet dies, it's at least given a decent burial and allowed to rest in peace. ("One Minute Interview" 81)

In real life Venus was not given a "decent burial," and her remains were exhibited for years at the Musée de l'Homme. Indeed, there were attempts to replace her with an understudy: Baartman died in 1815 at the age of twenty-six, and in 1829 another woman from the Khoisan tribe was displayed as the Hottentot Venus. According to Michele Wallace, "[S]he was the prize attraction at a ball given by Duchess du Barry in Paris" (31). This echoes the sense in the play, before Venus's death, that other scientists are in competition to produce Venuses of their own: the Grade-School Chum tells the Baron Docteur, "yr not the only Doc whos got hisself uh Hottentot . . . Some chap in Germany or somethin got his hands on one. He performed the autopsy today. Word is he'll publish inny minute" (142).

It is the dead Venus herself who recites a verse about the exhibition as the play is about to close (we hear an earlier, somewhat different version of this verse in the Overture):

Tail end of the tale for there must be uh end
is that Venus, Black Goddess, was shameless, she sinned or else
completely unknowing thuh Godfearin ways, she stood
showing her ass off in her iron cage.
When Death met Love Death deathd Love
and left Love tuh rot
au naturel end for thuh Miss Hottentot.

Loves soul, which was tidy, hides in heaven, yes, thats it
Loves corpse stands on show in museum. Please visit.

(161)

Therefore Venus, or the actress playing her, stands both inside and outside of the character at the end of the play; the audience witnesses Venus/Saartjie *both* as sympathetic figure and as historical entity. Her final words are a plea for the affection that Venus, named for the goddess of love, has sought and mistakenly thought she was receiving from the Baron Docteur. Parks has remarked, "I was drawn to her as a subject because of her name, Venus, love, and I write a lot about love in my work" (Chaudhuri,"For Posterior's Sake" 35). Here, Venus's words seem to turn toward the audience: "*Kiss* me *Kiss* me *Kiss* me *Kiss*" (162). As Lahr points out, "The Venus has to seduce because she has been abandoned—by the carnival world, by the Docteur, and, in a sense, by herself" (96). Her life is recycled with each performance of the text as it counts backward to her demise, only to begin again. The play's final moment of suspension, Venus's words of longing hanging in the air, leaves the audience in an uncomfortable space: true to Brechtian style, no catharsis is available. Instead of mourning Venus as heroine, we are left to consider the nature of spectatorial desire and its part in racist and colonialist practices.

Resurrecting Lincoln

The America Play and *Topdog/Underdog*

> Creswell, old fellow, everything is bright this morning. The war
> is over. It has been a tough time, but we have lived it out. Or
> some of us have. But it is over. We are going to have good times
> now, and a united country.
>
> —Abraham Lincoln, to Senator John Creswell, on April 14,
> 1865, the day he was assassinated (Thornton 200)

> "I take it you've discovered who started the riot,"
>   Anderson said.
> "We knew who he was all along," Grave Digger said.
> "It's just nothing we can do to him," Coffin Ed echoed.
> "Why not, for God's sake?"
> "He's dead," Coffin Ed said.
> "Who?"
> "Lincoln," Grave Digger said.
> "He hadn't ought to have freed us if he didn't want to make
>   provisions to feed us," Coffin Ed said. "Anyone could
>   have told him that."
>
> —Chester Himes, *Hot Day/Hot Night* (qtd. in Gates 96)

The America Play was written 1990–93 and opened at the Yale Repertory Theatre and then the New York Public Theater in 1994; *Topdog/Underdog* opened at the New York Public Theater in 2001 and transferred to Broadway's Ambassador Theater the following year. They were composed almost a decade apart, but it is natural to discuss them together because both "dig" into history by focusing on the figure of Abraham Lincoln. As with Hester Prynne in both *In the Blood* and *Fucking A*, Parks begins with an iconic character and rewrites that figure through the prism of African-American cultural history. She thus continues on the path followed in such earlier works as *Imperceptible Mutabilities in the Third Kingdom* and *The Death of the Last Black Man in the Whole Entire World*, questioning received, dominant—or invisible—narratives about black experience.

A number of recent studies of Lincoln have focused on aspects of his story that have previously been unexplored. Joshua Wolf Shenk, author of *Lincoln's Melancholy*, a book on his tendency toward depression, says, "He was someone who, according to those who knew him best and according to himself, was different. He suffered more, hurt more, struggled more. That was a big part of who Lincoln was. And we can't know him without knowing that" (qtd. in A. Gates B11). While Lincoln has traditionally been the man who freed the slaves, the century and a half since his death created a myth that tends to obscure problematic aspects of his political history. As Verna Foster points out, "The historical reception of Abraham Lincoln among African Americans has long been problematic. He has been both revered as the Great Emancipator and in the last half century or so criticized as a white supremacist"; she adds that Parks in interviews has said that she can see him as both (31). Katy Ryan begins her essay on *The America Play* by invoking a Frederick Douglass speech in which Douglass is openly critical of Lincoln; she quotes Douglass as saying, "Lincoln was not, in the fullest sense of the word, either our man or our model. In his interests, in his associations, in his habits of thought, and in his prejudices, he was a white man" (qtd. in Ryan 81). Not only is Lincoln a complex figure in African-American history, but Parks adds a metatheatrical twist by returning again and again in these two plays to the scene of Lincoln's assassination, which occurred while he was attending a performance of the farce *Our American Cousin*. The fact that the assassination took place while Lincoln was a spectator to a theatrical performance (and was assassinated by a failed actor) is of profound symbolic significance for this playwright whose own works call constant attention to images of performance and spectatorship.

The America Play

According to Parks, it took several years to create *The America Play*. "I wanted to write about a hole," she tells interviewer Michele Pearce (26). She began with the image of a mother and son digging for the remains of the father, and the turning point came when she felt as if someone had walked into the room and began talking to her: "I found the person I was looking for in the past. It was the Lincoln impersonator and that became the Lincoln Act" (qtd. in Fraden 46). Marc Robinson comments that *"The America Play* is both a story of a family (and its loss) and a nation (and *its* loss)" (191). The Lincoln of this play—another missing or absent father, as we saw in *Imperceptible Mutabilities*—is an African-American man, the "Foundling Father," who is told that he resembles the original and takes on the task of dressing up as Lincoln and being shot by various visitors to a penny arcade. In both this play and in *Topdog/Underdog*, Lincoln is impersonated by a black man; thus, Parks calls attention to both the specific interaction between African-Americans and this historical figure who "freed" them from slavery, and to the larger implications of acting or performing a character, particularly a historical character. While the two brothers of *Topdog/Underdog* have been abandoned by their parents, the name "Foundling Father" suggests that he is both linked to one of the *Founding* Fathers, and that he himself is a "foundling," or orphan.

The epigraph to the play, from John Locke, reads: "In the beginning, all the world was *America*" (159). Parks explains her thoughts behind this epigraph:

> Putting it at the beginning of the play and also in the program notes may encourage people to think about the *idea* of America in addition to the actual day-to-day reality of America. . . . All the world was an uncharted place, a blank slate, and since that beginning everyone's

been filling it with *tshatshkes,* which we who come next receive and must do something with. (Pearce 26)

Her imagery—the uncharted place (which becomes the hole), the *tshatshkes* (which become the Lincoln memorabilia and other artifacts in the theme park) is made manifest in the play itself.

Parks indicates in her opening stage directions that the play is set in "[a] great hole. In the middle of nowhere. The hole is an exact replica of The Great Hole of History" (158). This idea of a hole, a nowhere space, evokes the Beckettian no-places of *Waiting for Godot, Happy Days,* and other plays: it is both everywhere and nowhere at the same time, and indeed, *The America Play* has a Beckettian feeling of existing in a universe unto itself that parallels our own. As Parks herself has pointed out, the hole is also a womb space (she says in "Elements of Style," "People have asked me why I don't put any sex in my plays. 'The Great Hole of History'—like, duh" [16]). "From this fecund hole," Foster comments, "Parks (re)produces and reconstructs history" (28). It is a theater space into which the characters are born (echoing Pozzo's famous lines from *Godot,* "We give birth astride of a grave. The light gleams an instant, then it's night once more"). Una Chaudhuri echoes this awareness in her comment that the play "locates America where the theatrical imagination has long looked for it: a grave" (*Staging Place* 262). Responding to Chaudhuri, Robert Baker-White notes that America could be seen in this play as "both the hole itself and the material earth that has come out of it" (85). It is interesting that Parks calls the hole "an exact replica," suggesting that it is a simulacrum (we don't know where the "original" is, if there is one) that also evokes (especially in the Hall of Wonders of act 2) a Disneyification of history, embodied in the play itself in reenactments of the Lincoln assassination.

In this "Great Hole of History," our protagonist, the Foundling Father, tells us that he was "a Digger by trade. From a family of Diggers. Digged graves" (160). Parks thus places the "digger" up of the Lincoln story into the middle of her play, and the Lesser Known is also a character who "digs" (as in likes) history enough to make reliving it his vocation. The gravedigger links to the later character of the

Negro Resurrectionist in *Venus*, whose prior job was unearthing corpses for anatomists and who emcees the "resurrection" of the Venus Hottentot story; again, he is a surrogate author figure, excavating the past in order to re-member forgotten images. Finally, "Great Hole of History" sets up a paradoxical, postmodern pun. Much as some would like to see history as having a whole, that is, a contained presence (what Jean-François Lyotard would call a *grand récit*, or metanarrative), that presence is an impossibility or an absence—that is, a hole rather than a whole. This also echoes the idea in *Last Black Man* that history, particularly as it fails to tell the stories of submerged cultures, is an incomplete narrative. Multiple critics have been interested in Parks's hole of history as it affects African-American identity. In *Staging Whiteness*, Mary F. Brewer argues that it represents the specific absences of black narratives from white historical retellings:

> The hole symbolizes the erasure or distortion of Blacks in White historical narratives. It reflects too the practice of denying African Americans a recognizable U.S. parentage, so that, as orphans, Blacks do not inherit the same privileges as the nation's White descendants. What they inherit instead Parks calls "The Great Hole of History." (165)

Similarly, Louise Bernard cites Houston Baker's appropriation of the "black hole" image as a representation of black experience, a "subcultural (underground, marginal, or liminal) region in which a dominant, white culture's representations are squeezed to zero volume, producing a new expressive order" (qtd. in Bernard 689).

The text of act 1 is jammed with footnotes, not performed as in *Venus*, but scholarly amusements that fall somewhere between the erudite and the parodic. To some extent, Parks is parodying the research of traditional historical texts—yet she is also *showing* her own research. Some of these notes reflect received historical accounts, such as Lincoln's instructions to his troops to play "Dixie" at the end of the Civil War, Booth's last words, Robert E. Lee's last words, and Secretary of War Edwin Stanton's and First Lady Mary Todd Lincoln's words after the president was shot. Other footnotes, though, emphasize words like "possibly," "allegedly" and "probably," such as Mary's words after Lincoln's death, Booth's words to Lincoln as he shot him, or Mary's plea to her servant to bring in their son Tad. Kurt Bullock makes a fascinating argument for the ways that Parks thus "questions [the] legitimating authority" of "last words" (69). He adds that "[t]he lack of a final, transcendent statement by Lincoln" creates a "gap" that Parks opens (73). Parks tells us that the line she quotes from *Our American Cousin* is "very funny" and that Booth entered Lincoln's box and killed him as the audience was laughing (160). One footnote purports to come from a "composition . . . unpublished" (168) by the Foundling Father (i.e., her character) himself. In this way, Parks plays fast and loose with the intersections between documented and fictionalized or conjectured history. She thus reminds us that history itself is created via a series of perspectives and speculations.

In act 1, we see the "Foundling Father" (i.e., the black man dressed as Abraham Lincoln) narrating his own life and act, leading to his "assassination" at the end of the act by a Man playing John Wilkes Booth. Haike Frank calls our attention to his use of a third-person oral (auto)biographical form, as he "maintains the power of self-representation and articulates only what he wishes to reveal" (10). The Foundling Father refers to the "real" Lincoln as the Great Man, and to himself as the Lesser Known. The resemblance between the Lesser Known and the Great Man, he tells us repeatedly, was striking, with similarities in their height, thinness, long legs, hands and feet (though he does not mention that he is black and that Lincoln was white). The collection of beards that he carries around, he says, has required so much care that "he figured that the beards were completely his. Were as authentic as he was, so to speak" (160). To complete this costume, he has the initials "A.L." placed in gold lettering upon the box in which he keeps the beards. The Foundling Father's narration throughout the act is punctuated by two gestures, which he speaks (as if speaking stage directions aloud) and which are followed by the stage directions indicating the same gesture: a "wink to Mr. Lincolns pasteboard cutout" (160 and elsewhere), and a "nod to the bust of Mr. Lincoln" (161 and elsewhere). In a sense, this reinforces the play itself as nod or wink toward history, with the reminder that Lincoln himself is at this point primarily an icon, a statue or a cardboard cutout. For the character of the Foundling Father, the nod and wink are engagements with the character he is playing, as if he is both paying homage to Lincoln and upstaging him. Rayner and Elam emphasize the positioning of a black actor between these iconic images of the cutout and the bust; although their interpretation might be affected by the blocking of an actual production, they suggest that the center-stage placement of the Foundling Father demonstrates the way in which—despite his status in the margins of history—"his black body is purposefully and explicitly included" ("Echoes" 182). "The black actor," they add, "delivers his performance with a wink and a nod to the images of white history: undercutting them even while acknowledging them" (183). In Brechtian terms, the nod and wink are reminders to the audience of the separation between performer and character, just as we are made aware of the disjunction between the "historical" Lincoln and the Foundling Father's "replica" of him. Foster remarks, "As an event Lincoln's death (already literally theatrical in its origin and mythological in its reception) disappears in the Foundling Father's repeated performances of it" (30). Indeed, the Foundling Father comments, "It would be helpful to our story" (160) if he had ever met the Great Man, and fantasizes about being called to his side upon the assassination—but concludes that "none of this was meant to be" (161).

The Foundling Father explains that just as the log cabin was the shape around which the real Abraham Lincoln constructed the narrative of his life, he himself had a "favorite hole. A chasm, really" (162). This was the theme park that he and his wife Lucy once visited, which contained pageants and replicas of the great figures of history. Ever since the day he saw it, the images of "Reconstructed Historicities" have been parading before him "in his minds eye" (163). The word *reconstructed* calls attention not only to Parks's favored images of re-membering and of histories—"historicities"—themselves as constructions, but also to the Reconstruction after the Civil War. The hole of the theme park is a chasm, an abyss, because history itself is a *mise-en-abîme* into which the past has fallen. A hole is, paradoxically, both a shape and a container of emptiness; the Foundling Father wants to be able to give his own past a shaping image just as the "Great Man" did. This is why, he says, he went out West and to create "his own Big Hole" (163); at the end of his work day of gravedigging, he would perform his Lincoln imitation, but did-n't make any money until he invited the crowds to throw old food at him. This created enough of a draw that he began to perform his act in small towns. When someone remarked that he "played Lincoln so well that he ought to be shot" (164), he was inspired to return to his hole and—instead of imitating Lincoln's speeches—to reenact the assassination. As a result, "The Lesser Known became famous overnight" (164). Frank suggests that the public's "greater interest in Lincoln's murder than in his political speeches and, by implication, his political deeds" reflects "the dominance of fragmentation and the power of sensationalism in society"; she argues that the fascination with repetition is like our immersion in television re-presentations of moments of disaster (12).

The Foundling Father's narrative is followed by an example of his reenactment, wherein a man pretending to be John Wilkes Booth enters at the moment that Lincoln (played by the Foundling Father) is guffawing at a joke during the performance of *Our American Cousin*, points a gun at his head, and says Booth's famous words, "Thus to the tyrants" (and sometimes also "The South is avenged!"), and Lincoln/the Foundling Father "slumps in his chair" (165). At the end of the demonstration, the man who has played Booth thanks the Foundling Father politely and both of them say, "Till next week" (165). The Foundling Father explains that this particular Booth, who comes every week, "always chooses the Derringer" though he is offered several kinds of guns, and that the ones who choose this one "are the ones for History . . . By the book" (166). As she will repeat in *Topdog/Underdog*, Parks uses tourists who want to act out the part of Booth in the assassination of Lincoln—and the complicity, even profit, of the Lincoln impersonator—to comment on the reduction of history to a kind of cultural tourism that prioritizes the thrills of revenge and death over the real moments of bodily trauma or the political implications of the assassination itself. The tourists are would-be actors imitating the failed actor Booth, but like Booth, derive a feeling of power from "making" history happen. The Lincoln impersonator earns money and fame from the act, but he also allows himself to be violated. The continuous repetition of the assassination, week after week with different and returning customers—like repeated performances of a play in which the protagonist must die—places the act itself into a *mise-en-abîme*, a Beckettian void or bottomless hole. Bullock remarks that this repeated assassination is a "ritual" and a "way of disrupting history": "Finding the assassination simulation empty, absent of meaning, the ritual is repeated and repeated, much like the quotations of 'last words' are used over and over" (77). Chaudhuri takes the effect of the repetition-as-ritual a step further and characterizes it as one that celebrates "the violence at the heart of American history" (*Staging Place* 264).

The Foundling Father also mentions sometimes wearing a yellow beard instead of a black one because "[s]ome inaccuracies are good for business" (168), adding that people prefer him to wear his stovepipe hat even though Lincoln would not have kept it on indoors: "[P]eople dont like their Lincoln hatless" (168). What he realizes, as an impersonator, is that the historical persona is a constructed image; accuracy is less important than reinforcing a persona. As S.E. Wilmer notes, "The nature of the theatrical space and the acting profession is parodied when the Foundling Father endeavours to gain renown by acting like someone else" (447). Even the "slight deafness" in one ear (169) that he says is the only side effect he suffers (as the result of the gunshots) reflects the sense in which the decision to create his character involves both an awareness of the past and a willingness to turn a deaf ear on certain aspects of it (or perhaps on the implications of what he is doing).

What fascinates the Foundling Father most is the distance of twenty feet that separated the president's theater box from the stage where *Our American Cousin* was being played, as well as "the time it took the murderer to cross that expanse, and how the murderer crossed it. He jumped" (168). He does not say why this interests him so much, but the space and time he describes here is another chasm, a literalization of the distance between audience and playing space, a distance that is violated once Booth leaps into Lincoln's box and again from there to the stage. Rayner and Elam suggest that this twenty-foot distance is "a precise measurement for the immeasurable distance between theatrical illusion and the historical fact" ("Echoes" 184). In other words, the Foundling Father is intent on that gap between spectator and performer, and on what it means to bridge or violate that gap. His investment in what he later calls "[t]he passage of time. The crossing of space" (170) also suggests his need—perhaps engendered in part by his awareness of mortality through having formerly been a gravedigger—for posterity, for continuing the past into the present. He describes Lincoln as having lived in a "pastland" that is "somewhere 'back there'" (171) and about his own quest to become just as memorable by following in Lincoln's footsteps even though these footsteps (since Lincoln lived in the past) are actually behind him. This imagination of history's posteriority (which was, of course, also Parks's preoccupation in *Venus*) culminates in the Foundling Father's fantasy about moving backward into death and thus having the Greater Man catch up to him, wrestle him to the ground, and even repeat "Death to the tyrants!" as he leaves the Lesser Known (i.e., the Foundling Father) on the ground and continues in his place. The act seems to be both the revenge he feels he deserves at the hands of Lincoln, and a fantasy of letting himself be eclipsed by the mythic figure whom he so admires.

The second act of the play, "The Hall of Wonders," features Lucy and Brazil (the Foundling Father's widow and son) in the replica of the Great Hole of History, in the "middle of nowhere" (174). Lucy (who shares a name with Parks's paternal grandmother) has taken on the Foundling Father's semideafness (she has an ear trumpet and, as Frank says, is "straining to hear the echo of history" [18]), while Brazil has taken on his role as digger. Rayner and Elam comment on the connection between the first and second acts: "Just as the Foundling Father in the first act seeks recovery of an identity through repetition of the Lincoln scene, Lucy and Brazil, in the second act, seek recovery of the body of the dead Foundling Father" ("Echoes" 181). As the act begins, the sounds of gunshots echo loudly; this is both an echo from the past (the Foundling Father's assassination routine) and another image of repetition. Lucy tells Brazil about his father's "lonely death and lack of burial" (175), implying that he never achieved the kind of fame that he longed for so deeply. She recounts to him the story of Bram Price, a boy (perhaps a former love of hers) who died and then came back and sat down for dinner; another Parksian image of resurrection, this ghost seems to provide the impetus for Lucy to compare her own story with that of the Prices. The mother, Miz Penny Price, apparently was full of secrets and "wore red velvet in August" (175); she was a harlot who "sold herself" (176) after both her husband and her son died. When Miz Price herself went mad and then also died—perhaps under questionable circumstances—Brazil says that he "gnashed" for her (176) until he chipped a tooth.

He seems to have taken on the business of professional undertaker or mourner performing grief: "I woulda tore at my coat but that's extra" (176)—thus resembling his father. Rayner and Elam point out the connections between Brazil's "fakin" and black cultural practices that create forms of subversion: "The showmanship in acting out mourning parodies rituals from the performative black church tradition as well as from the minstrel tradition of stereotype, exaggeration, and exploitation . . . African American minstrels could both mock and profit from the dominant culture. Brazil's skill in imitating kept the money pouring in" ("Echoes" 189–90). In this sense, we can see a clear connection between Ham's ancestry speech in *Last Black Man* and Brazil's performance of mourning.

Unlike his father, though, Brazil seems to be digging for the sake of finding items to add to their "Hall of Wonders"; he is an archaeologist of sorts as well as an entrepreneur. Foster comments that Brazil "finds, not the father he is seeking, but historical artifacts, reproductions and symbols" (29). Buried items are equated with secrets, such as when Lucy tells Brazil that the senior Bram Price wore lifts in his shoes but that this was a deathbed confession of his that she has kept to herself for nineteen years. This makes Brazil wonder if it would be possible for them to dig up his father's bones and in turn to find out *his* deathbed confessions, his "whispers" (178), but Lucy cautions that since it has been thirty years since they have seen him, there could be some difficulties (the different movement of the whispers in the West, or some kind of technical "interference" [178]) that prevent the two from hearing them.

Brazil refers to the Foundling Father as his "foe-father" (178), with the obvious pun on *forefather* that later in the play transmutes into "faux-father" (184). He describes his early childhood as being part of a sort of funeral con team, with dad doing the digging (but for whom "fakin was his callin'"), his mother as the "Confidence," and his own job being to do "thuh weepin and thuh moanin" (179). Brazil brags that even though it was embarrassing to have his father die alone without a proper burial, he was originally such an amazing digger that he was the one who dug the Great Hole of History replica in which they now find themselves, a copy of the original one where his mother and father had their honeymoon. Although he was obviously not there himself, he explains how, on their honeymoon, Lucy and the Foundling Father would sit and watch the parades of great ones go by, including another father figure, the "father of the country" George Washington, who would rise up from the dead (yet another resurrection image). Lucy is quick to correct her son, explaining that the Washington they saw was "uh lookuhlike" and that the real one is long since dead (179). Brazil seems to be confused about the difference, and Lucy urges him to remember that the Hole was "uh theme park son. Keep your story to scale" (180). Ryan comments that "[k]eeping the story to scale is precisely the difficulty when one is dealing with history, whether familial or national" (89).

After enumerating more of the greats that his parents would see— everyone from activist Marcus Garvey to pop culture icon Tarzan— Brazil remarks that Lincoln was his father's favorite, and goes on to imitate his father's imitation of Lincoln dropping dead. Lucy comments on what a splendid "faker" the Foundling Father was; clearly, both of them are enamored of the legend they have created about him as a consummate faker or actor. She even teaches Brazil to copy the cry that his father would make just to get his audience's attention, and encourages him to go ahead and dig. Brazil reminisces about how, when he was only a very small child, the Foundling Father taught him the types of performances that he would need to know in order to continue his father's craft of being a digger/faker: the "Wail," the "Weep," the "Sob," the "Moan," the right ways to stand during the "Mourning Moment," and the "Gnash" (182). This image of the son resurrecting the father is followed immediately both by Brazil digging up the bust of Lincoln (which they will put in their Hall of Wonders), and by an excerpt from *Our American Cousin* (the play by Tom Taylor that Lincoln was watching at the time of his assassination) in which the character of Mr. Trenchard finds the place where his father kept all of his old deeds. It is worth noting that the excerpts throughout are performed by black actors in whiteface in a kind of reverse minstrelsy (and that the Foundling Father, in the second act, is one of the players); as Jeanette Malkin puts it, doing so additionally "underscores the absence of blacks within the American historical imagination" (176). These sequences reiterate Parks's idea that history perpetuates itself through simulacra, and that each generation is called upon to imitate the previous one without questioning the nature of the falsehoods or performances involved. Brazil's reverence for his father's calling, and his desire to imitate it, is touching, but it also bespeaks a willful misunderstanding about the past; what is left are the attitudes and poses, the souvenirs and the artifacts.

As he muses on the nature of history and on what has come before them, Brazil refers to the Great Hole as their "inheritance of sorts" (185); Parks will take up this theme of legacies and inheritances more fully in *Topdog/Underdog*. There is some tension between him and his mother, played out in a long "spell" between them at this juncture. She wants him to keep digging, but he becomes increasingly absorbed in showing off his ability to imitate his father, pretending that he is emceeing an introduction to the wonders in the collection (a box with *A.L.* on it, Washington's wooden teeth, the bust of Lincoln, etc.) while his mother admonishes him again to "keep it tuh scale" (185). Instead of listening to her, Brazil builds a monologue (almost a performance poem) in which he enumerates a laundry list of artifacts and documents. This mutates into a list of medals for accomplishments and skills: "horseback riding, swimmin, croquet and badminton. Community Service. For cookin and for cleanin. For bowin and scrapin. Uh medal for fakin? Huh. This could uh been his" (186). With his speech, despite his mother's warnings, Brazil shows an actorly bravado in his own right; it also shows the detritus of the past as both trivial and essential. He shows no ability to distinguish between the concrete and the abstract. By the same token, Brazil's loud weeping immediately after this is both a real act of mourning for his father and a demonstration of his ability (learned from his father) to *perform* grief. He has been successful in the sense that his mother, at least, feels ready to bequeath the father's spade to him, as she does shortly afterward, telling him that he looks more and more like the Foundling Father every day.

Right before Lucy does this, in a rather hallucinatory sequence, another excerpt from *Our American Cousin* appears, only this time one of the characters, Mrs. Mount, is played by the Foundling Father. He interrupts this staging to perform bits from his own act (it is not clear whether this sequence is something Lucy and Brazil can see, or imagine seeing, or whether it is just for us in the audience): the Gettysburg Address, the naming of the U.S. capitals. Interestingly, when he goes on to offer what he says will be the "centerpiece of the evening" (188), his narrative of the death of Lincoln is done in a way that mixes up, repeats, and confuses the chronological events: "the slipping of Booth into the presidential box unseen, the freeing of the slaves, the pulling of the trigger . . ." (189). Frank points out that he tells the story "as if he were describing the individual pictures of a comic strip" (14). As the events themselves fall into the Great Hole of History, each phrase has an iconic meaning for the Foundling Father's spectators, and yet they seem to want a potpourri of narratives (each line is like a tag or reminder) reiterated for their pleasure without much concern about accuracy.

As Brazil continues to dig, he finds a trumpet, a bag of pennies (with, of course, Lincoln on them), and the yellow beard. This is accompanied by Lucy's litanies, first of well-known American sayings (she conflates Lincoln's phrases with those of other famous figures like P. T. Barnum), and then of expressions for how she felt about her husband ("the bees knees," etc. [193]). She calls these her "re-memberies" (194), again invoking one of Parks's variations on the word that combines an act of memory with an act of putting something back together again. At the same time, Brazil digs up a television, and the Foundling Father's face appears on it in a replay of the "Lincoln act" (though without working sound). Interestingly, in this now doubly mediated version of the assassination, Brazil is particularly aware of the fact that his father is "[o]nly fakin" (195)—that is, performing. While they are watching, the Foundling Father (in the flesh) shows up and presents himself in front of his coffin. "He's dead?" asks Brazil (who seems to be confused about the translations between image and reality), and Lucy responds that he is, adding casually that Brazil should turn off the television and asking her husband (as if she were asking about something as mundane as taking a shower) about the coffin: "You gonna get in now or later?" (196). The Foundling Father says that he wants to wait, but twice when he asks for a hug, Lucy and Brazil say that they are not yet ready to give him one; it is as if they are unprepared to deal with him, and there are several spell sequences here where the three of them regard one another and we then hear both the gunplay sound effects and Lucy's story about the Great Hole again.

When Lucy urges her husband to do his Lincoln routine for Brazil, he obliges with a combined version of his various bits, culminating in the enacted assassination. This time, though, he really does seem to be dead. We find out for the first time, from Brazil, that Lucy herself was also a child performer, labeled a Confidence at the age of eight when her uncle died and she refused to tell her family his last words. In this sense, then, we realize that Brazil has inherited the trade of mourning/performance from both of his parents. When he asks Lucy if it is time now for him to "gnash," she replies that it would be better for him to "save it for thuh guests" (199). The play ends, then, with Brazil doing his patter to announce the items in the Great Hall of Wonders, including the jewel box, the wooden teeth, and the aforementioned list of medals with their rather surreal list of Boy Scout–like activities, again culminating in "For bowin and scrapin. A medal for fakin" (199). Strikingly, though, he closes both his speech and the play itself by introducing the Foundling Father's body as part of the display:

Note: thuh body sitting propped upright in our great Hole. Note the large mouth opened wide. Note the top hat and frock coat, just like the greats. Note the death wound: thuh great black hole—thuh great black hole in thuh great head.—And how this great head is bleedin.—Note: thuh last words.—And thuh last breaths.—And how thuh nation mourns—(*Takes his leave*) (199)

As Bullock suggests, Parks implies that "the grave can never be a site of rest" (84). Ryan adds, "Returned from the 'dead' to enter another grave, the Foundling Father quickly becomes a spectacle, a commodity, buried in another narrative, as the nation mourns" (90). Brazil's utter displacement from the sense that the dead man was his father is evident in his objectifying the body as part of their display; it is reduced to "the large mouth," "the top hat and frock coat," and so forth without even a "his" attached. More than that, the "great black hole" is now evident in the Foundling Father's head. Parks thus paints a picture of the black man's wounding in history, the use of the Lincoln myth to create a fake version of liberation and valor at the expense of the real pain and suffering of blacks, which is swallowed into a black hole of forgetting and replaced by commodification and theatricality. There is undoubtedly a sense of pride in his legacy in Brazil's performance, yet it is also being done for the *sake* of performance—which is itself an act of "re-membering," but also a kind of selective forgetting.

Topdog/Underdog

Parks takes up some of the same themes and images in *Topdog/Underdog* that she does in *The America Play*. When she won the 2002 Pulitzer Prize for *Topdog/Underdog*, it became time to worry that the dramatist had sold out by leaving the avant-garde and entering the Broadway mainstream, the Broadway of *The Full Monty* and *The Lion King*. After winning the Pulitzer, Parks was interviewed by *People* magazine, and expressed excitement at the wide audience that *Topdog* was garnering: "I love seeing the old hard-core theatergoers and the kids who have their baseball hats backward . . . We've got all kinds of people sitting there loving the play" (Miller and

Cotliar 143–44). Elizabeth Pochoda echoed this excitement in her review in *The Nation:* "Even if [the play's] success were to be measured solely by the numbers of young people and black people, both young and old, in the audience on any given night, *Topdog* could be considered a healthy sign" (36). Ben Brantley of the *New York Times* called the work "the most exciting new home-grown play to hit Broadway since . . . *Angels in America,*" and expressed some surprise that such an "entertaining wallop" could come from "a woman who [previously] wrote defiantly nonlinear dramas with intimidating titles" (1). Coming from the opposite direction, Una Chaudhuri's review of the play in *Theatre Journal* expresses some surprise that Parks seems to have headed in the direction of "psychological realism" (albeit in a reinvented form), but ultimately concludes that Parks's "expansive new American dramaturgy" is "not restricted to the so-called experimental modes of theatre" (289, 291). The play, which also earned Parks several Tony nominations, among other awards, thrust Parks into the national limelight as a dramatist whose enigmatic, deeply political, and poetic works had been staged off-Broadway and regionally for just over a decade.

The success of this second Lincoln play marked a startling contrast to the initial media reception to *The America Play,* as the Public Theater production had received mixed reviews. John Simon of *New York Magazine* called it "a farrago of undigested Beckett and distantly ogled Joyce," and Markland Taylor of *Variety* thought it suffered from "the emperor's-new-clothes syndrome" (both qtd. in Backalenick 27). Vincent Canby in the *New York Times* admired the "physical production" of the play but judged that it "lessened the playwright's obligation" to create a work that "could be played with as much effect in the middle of an ordinary living room" (qtd. in Garrett 133). In a sense, Parks takes Canby's criticism to heart in *Topdog/Underdog;* explaining that the piece came "right out of" *The America Play,* she says, "[W]hile I envision *The America Play* taking place in a vast void, *Topdog* is set in a seedy, furnished room" (Garrett 134). Chaudhuri calls this set "not just a room, but an archetypal room, a room with a vengeance . . . [and the] very emblem of limits and boundaries" (289).

It is true that *Topdog/Underdog* is more "accessible" than most of Parks's earlier works. The play creates virtuoso performances by using just two actors, who portray Lincoln (Jeffrey Wright in the off-Broadway and Broadway productions) and Booth (Don Cheadle off-Broadway and the rapper Mos Def on Broadway). These two figures are brothers (their names were given to them by their father as a joke, we are told); Lincoln is a reformed card shark who is now an Abraham Lincoln impersonator, and Booth is attempting to learn how to deal cards the way his brother used to. What follows is a relatively straightforward tragicomedy that ends with one brother killing the other. I want to argue, however, that Parks has not stepped off the powerful artistic platform of her earlier works. Rather, there is a strong continuity in terms of performative issues, language, and themes such as ancestry, violence, and commodification.

As in virtually all of Parks's other theater pieces, the characters in *Topdog* play performers, and as such there is a constant metadramatic quality that informs the work by raising issues of display, identity, and masking central to an African-American aesthetic. As the play begins, while Booth is attempting to learn the art of one kind of performance, the three-card monte deal, Lincoln has abandoned the cards (after his friend Lonny, his "Stickman," was killed) for the rather unusual job of dressing up as Abraham Lincoln for an amusement gallery and letting tourists "assassinate" him on a daily basis. His costume for the impersonation includes a top hat and dress clothes as well as a beard and whiteface makeup. Part of the tyranny of the position involves not only having to pay for and take care of his own costume (and getting in trouble when he tears his beard), but the humiliating "mask" created by the white makeup. One might situate this reverse blackface in the tradition of such works as Jean Genet's *The Blacks* and other plays more directly critical of the minstrel tradition such as Ntozake Shange's *Spell* #7. Here, Parks creates her own version of a trope that appears frequently in African-American literature: that African-American identity almost inevitably involves disguise and role-playing as part of the effort to function in a hostile culture. Brantley suggests that the play, with its emphasis on "the existential traps of being African-American and male in the

United States, the masks that wear the men as well as vice versa," is "all about poses and pretenses, large and small" and about "life as a series of theatrical postures: some voluntary, some reflexive and some imposed by centuries of history" (1, 3).

Like Parks's other works, *Topdog* makes use of "spells," which are particularly potent in a play that features only two characters because of the intensity of the unspoken transactions between them. For example, there is a lengthy "Lincoln/Booth/Lincoln/Booth" spell right after Booth says to Lincoln, "Maybe yll show me yr moves sometime" (63); a director might imaginatively fill this moment with the sense of how Booth wants something that Lincoln doesn't want to give him. Parks also marks the piece with a chorus of sorts, as she does in so many of her plays; here, it is the patter associated with the dealing of the cards. The play is punctuated by the lines of the three-card monte routine, which reappears during almost every scene; Lincoln's version of it is smooth as silk, "deft, dangerous, electric," as Parks puts it (55), designed after years of practice to take the listener in:

> (((Lean in close and watch me now: who see thuh black card who see the black card I see thuh black card black cards thuh winner pick thuh black card thats thuh winner pick thuh red card thats thuh loser. (55)

Booth's attempts at the patter are, "for the most part, studied and awkward" (5). Again, there is a musicality and a "rep and rev" to the choruses in this play. But the three-card "chorus" takes on two additional forms of resonance. First, Booth's version of it is imperfect, a rehearsal, and we see the connection to his status as an actor (like the original Booth?) learning his role. One is reminded of the scene in *Venus* in which we get to eavesdrop on Venus "practicing" the way she would order the servants around if she were rich. Second, the three-card monte game itself is predicated on this hypnotic patter, designed to put the street audience under its spell, just as this choral version of it becomes the set piece—the source of enchantment—of the play. As in *Venus* (though certainly not to the same degree), the spectators are implicated as willing, fascinated consumers. As Margo Jefferson puts it, "[T]he fact that we could be in the street or the subway watching this act is titillating. So is the game itself. No bogus stage tricks at the Ambassador Theater; this actor has to handle the cards, and by watching, we become the potential suckers or the too-smart-for-that bystanders" (9).

In the case of Booth, the longing to be an impressive performer also extends to various kinds of self-deception. One manifestation of this is his insistence on his power over his girlfriend Grace (who, notably, the audience never sees; one might say that "grace" is absent from this play). He attempts to convince both himself and his brother that Grace is desperately in love with him, saying that he has boosted her a ring that's half a size too small "so she cant just take it off on a whim, like she did the last one I gave her" (8). He brags to Lincoln in scene 3 that Grace allowed him to have sex with her without a rubber, and Lincoln asks for a detailed description but knows his brother well enough to think he is lying, an accusation that infuriates Booth, who replies: "You a limp dick jealous whiteface motherfucker whose wife dumped him cause he couldnt get it up and she told me so. Came crawling to me cause she needed a man" (43). In one scene, he creates an entire setting of a romantic dinner with champagne, fancy stolen dishes, and the like, only to wind up insisting at four in the morning that she'll be there any minute.

Connected to Booth's sexual frustration and to his deeply ingrained rivalry with his brother is his attempt to become as skilled as Lincoln at cards. Although he is still a rather inept dealer, Booth insists to Lincoln that he is changing his name to 3-Card, as if putting on the new moniker will change his fate. Booth yearns to impress Lincoln, to show that he is as capable a dealer as Lincoln himself once was, but he masks his ineptitude with a bravado that suggests his longing for the trappings of success (money, Grace, etc.) has overpowered his ability to gauge how he is really being received. When Lincoln offers Booth the services of his three-card monte crew, it is clear that Lincoln misses the old days even though he has given up the game, and he fantasizes about introducing Booth by saying he'd "been working the west coast. Little towns. Mexican border.

Taking tourists" (45). At the same time, Booth resents Lincoln's power and claims that he is perfectly capable of finding his own crew, though later in the same scene Booth imagines that if Lincoln were to get fired, they would be able to work the three-card monte game together; he asks Lincoln to show him "the hook part of the hustle," but Lincoln refuses (51).

When Lincoln finally agrees to help Booth and the two engage in a sort of rehearsal, Lincoln details the various roles: "Theres thuh Dealer, thuh Stickman, thuh Sides, thuh Lookout and thuh Mark. I'll be thuh Dealer" (71). Booth, ignoring the impracticality of the role since they are not actually out on the street, says eagerly that he wants to be the Lookout and that he even has his gun on him; Lincoln finally persuades him that in order to learn the game, Booth should be the Side. In one of the play's metadramatic sequences, they "rehearse" such things as sizing up the crowd Lincoln, the expert performer, explains that the Dealer has to act as if he doesn't want to play. He tells Booth that pulling off the con (just as is the case for an actor) is all about attitude, about combining the "moves and the grooves, thuh talk and the walk, thuh patter and the pitter pat, thuh flap and thuh rap: what yr doing with yr mouth and what yr doing with yr hands" (74). When he hands the cards over to Booth so that he can practice dealing, he tells him to give them a light touch, "[l]ike yr touching Graces skin" (78). In a way, though, the connection is too threatening for Booth (since this rehearsal occurs while Grace has stood him up), and he reaches for his gun (and has to be calmed down) when Lincoln laughs at his ineptitude with the cards; clearly, Booth thinks his masculinity as a "performer" is at stake.

In one scene that is a theatrical tour de force, Booth comes in wearing the two full suits that he has "boosted" for himself and for Lincoln, one on top of the other, and we see the amazing intricacy of his shoplifting skill as he removes and displays all of the items of clothing in a kind of vaudeville bit. This is followed by a Ma and Pa Kettle act that Lincoln and Booth have made into their comic ritual every time that Lincoln brings home his pay: they take a drink together, apportion the money with elaborate gestures, and go through their routine: "Dont die on me, Ma!" says Lincoln, to which

Booth responds, "Im fading fast, Pa!" (24). As with Lincoln's earlier blues song, their routine is comic yet picks up imagery from their actual family situation. Lincoln, on the other hand, uses an awareness of the fakeness of his act as his survival strategy. He tells Booth:

> They say the clothes make the man. All day long I wear that getup. But that dont make me who I am. Old black coat not even real old just fake old. . . . Dust from the cap guns on the left shoulder where they shoot him, where they shoot me I should say but I never feel like they shooting me. . . . Worn suit coat, not even worn by the fool that Im supposed to be playing, but making fools out of all those folks who come crowding in for they chance to play at something great. Fake beard. Top hat. Dont make me into no Lincoln. I was Lincoln on my own before any of that. (27–28)

Whereas the Foundling Father in *The America Play* uses the costume to his advantage—even variations like the yellow beard—and seems to create a self out of his act, Lincoln distances himself from the figure he is playing, claiming an identity that comes from within rather than from the figure he is playing. He has a "Best Customer" who visits the arcade repeatedly and whispers things to Lincoln (before shooting him) like "Yr only yrself—when no ones watching" (32). Booth and Lincoln wonder whether the man is "a brother" (they think so), thus adding to the play's imagery of brother-on-brother violence, but Lincoln says that he doesn't mind the interaction because the man "makes the day interesting" (33). While he and Booth agree that the things the man says are "deep," they are untroubled and unreflective because the exchange is just part of the routine, part of the act. Afterward, we see Lincoln putting on his costume "like an actor preparing for a great role" (35). When Booth wonders whether Lincoln ever worries that an arcade customer will use a real gun on him, Lincoln replies that he doesn't and that he is not supposed to be looking at the visitors: "Im supposed to be staring straight ahead. Watching a play, like Abe was" (47). But then he admits that he can see an upside-down reflection of the customers on the metal electrical box on the opposite wall, and he draws Booth into his narrative about what the ritual assassinations feel like:

Thuh gun is always cold. Winter or summer thuh gun is always cold. And when the gun touches me he can feel that Im warm and he knows Im alive. And if Im alive then he can shoot me dead. And for a minute, with him hanging back there behind me, its real. Me looking at him upside down and him looking at me looking like Lincoln. Then he shoots . . . More come in. Uh whole day full . . . I do my best for them. And now they talking bout replacing me with uh wax dummy. Itll cut costs. (48)

Although he claimed earlier that dressing up as Lincoln doesn't make him into Lincoln, this speech suggests the moment, each time, at which the act becomes real to him; playing dead seems to make him feel more alive in a way that Booth has not found for himself. At this point, Booth insists that Lincoln could jazz up his act by making his death seem more extreme, and they rehearse gestures of exaggerated groaning and falling (Booth encourages Lincoln to "curse" and to "practice rolling and wiggling on the floor" [49]). This "rehearsal" also rather unnervingly foreshadows Lincoln's actual death (at Booth's hands) at the end of the play, which is also prefigured by Booth "shooting" Lincoln's picture (90); perhaps Lincoln, in his speech, has unwittingly revealed the seductiveness of the assassin's power. As Booth "directs" Lincoln in how to play out the assassination more convincingly, he tells him, "And look at me! I am the assassin! *I am Booth!!* Come on man this is life and death! Go all out!" (50). It is at this point, though, after "going all out," that Lincoln stops him and says that the act is looking "too real" (50). Despite the moments of actual physical warmth and cold, he needs to remind himself that this is a "sit down job. With benefits" (51), wherein he is a performer and con artist (just as he was a performer and con artist as a three-card monte dealer), yet the price of doing so is not to question the implications of the act too much. Booth, on the other hand, lacks both Lincoln's concentration and his distance; to him, the show-and-tell (the outward display, the narration) of an act is what makes it real.

When Lincoln is alone shortly afterward, we see him picking up a deck of cards, which he "studies . . . like an alcoholic would study a drink" (55). He is caught between the agency that being a con artist gave him, and the fear that staying in the life will eventually kill him the way that it killed Lonny. Not much later, he is fired, though, replaced by a "wax dummy" that is "right out of a catalog" (60). To the arcade owners, there is little difference between Lincoln's imitation Lincoln and a mannequin, though to Lincoln himself the job—humiliating though it is—is what is keeping him from the danger he fears he will place himself in if he returns to hustling the cards. After he has "rehearsed" the three-card monte game in order to help Booth, though, he is left shuffling the cards, and when we see him at the beginning of the play's final scene, he is exultant because he has just returned from winning big-time at the cards and tells himself, "I got my shit back" (84). Unbeknownst to him, though, Booth has been watching part of his monologue, and hence his own "news" that Grace asked *him* to marry *her* seems to be part of his effort to compete with his brother, especially since Lincoln claims to have no news of his own other than that he has a new job as a security guard (we never find out whether this is true).

A key theme of *Topdog* that echoes Parks's earlier works is one of legacies and inheritances, lineage and the recording (and sometimes misremembering) of history. As Robinson says of *Last Black Man* and *The America Play*—but which could easily be asserted of *Topdog* as well—"the characters of Parks's theater are always hoping better to understand their relation to their inheritance" (191). The first kind of history that *Topdog* traffics in is a familial one. One of the main sources of bonding between Lincoln and Booth is their telling of stories about their parents and their mutual speculation about why they were abandoned (first by their mother, when the brothers were sixteen and thirteen, and two years later by their father as well). Foster points out that in this sense, the brothers are "foundlings" like the Foundling Father (33). Booth says that one day he cut school and caught their mother "putting her stuff in bags" (19); at one point, they wonder if their parents simply went somewhere else and started a different family: "Maybe they got 2 new kids. 2 boys. Different than us, though. Better"(69). The two brothers look through their family photo album and agree that although they never did the pastoral childhood activities like selling lemonade in the summer that Lincoln at first pretends they did, they are unified in their memories of moments like the practical joke they played on their father by putting nails under his tires, and conspiring to keep cool while he railed about "how thuh white man done sabotaged him again" (64). Parks shows us simultaneously the painfulness of their memories and the sense that even so, they are what unify Lincoln and Booth as brothers: their shared past, their legacy, along with the rituals they have devised to entertain themselves, keep them going. At this point, their bonding comes through the stories they have left to tell as they try to figure out why both of their parents were so unhappy; Lincoln says, "I think there was something out there that they liked more than they liked us and for years they was struggling against moving towards that more liked something. Each of them had a special something that they was struggling against" (66).

As we have seen, the same might be said for the two sons as well. Theirs is a legacy of confusion and betrayal, when Lincoln tells Booth that their father used to bring him along on visits to various women (one of whom was willing to have sex with Lincoln himself as well), Booth narrates a story about sleeping with Lincoln's wife (Cookie), "[r]ight in that bed" (92). In a rare moment of self-disclosure informed by their shared past, Booth describes this to Lincoln as "[t]hat bad part of me that I fight down everyday. You beat yrs down and it stays there dead but mine keeps coming up for another round" (92). Earlier, Lincoln sings a blues song that he says he made up and that follows a familiar blues pattern, but its content (his mother left him, his father left him, his woman left him, all that's left is "a hearse" [21]) mirrors the situation of the plot itself. Foster suggests that there is a connection between Lincoln's identification with his father and his Abraham Lincoln impersonation:

> Talking about his Lincoln costume leads him to remember the clothes his father left hanging in the closet when he left home; instead of wearing his father's clothes, Linc burnt them and subsequently wore a fake version of Abraham Lincoln's clothes instead. . . . In symbolic terms, he has abandoned and wasted his African her-

itage and become complicit in the Anglo-American version of history personified by Lincoln. When he loses his job, he is displaced from this tradition too. (34)

We find out that Booth and Lincoln, before being left on their own by their parents, were each given a wad of money in a stocking and told not to tell the other brother about it. The money, referred to as their "inheritance" throughout the play, becomes first a point of memory and legacy. Booth, an adept shoplifter, will steal for worldly goods or do without a phone, but he puts aside the wadded-up stocking that his mother gave him and refuses to open or spend it. The climactic event of the play occurs when Booth, who has insisted on having Lincoln deal a three card monte game to him because he thinks he can guess the cards (and he has done so in their prior rehearsal, probably because Lincoln let him), bets and loses his "inheritance" to Lincoln. Strikingly, just before Booth turns over the (wrong) card, Lincoln asks him, "You think we're really brothers?" (102). The question may be in response to Booth's story about knowing their mother was cheating on their father. But it is also perhaps an act of gamesmanship to distract him. Booth responds that he believes they are brothers, and this is followed by a "spell" between them, after which Booth, his concentration broken, points to the incorrect card. Although Lincoln insists that he is "just laughing," not laughing *at* Booth (104), Booth feels belittled. While trying to cut open the stocking, Lincoln tells him:

> [T]huh first move is to know that there aint no winning. It may look like you got a chance but the only time you pick right is when thuh man lets you. And when its thuh real deal, when its thuh real fucking deal, bro, and thuh moneys on thuh line, thats when thuh man wont want you picking right. (106)

Even though Lincoln thinks he is simply addressing the matter of the three-card monte game, to Booth these words suggest his lack of control over his own fate. We learn that instead of having a genuine reason to celebrate Grace's acceptance of his marriage proposal, Booth has apparently shot her for rejecting him. The threat posed to his masculinity by Grace's refusal plays itself out in her giving back his ring: "She werent wearing my ring I gived her. Said it was too small. Fuck that. Said it hurt her. Fuck that. Said she was into bigger things. *Fuck* that" (107). In response, Lincoln tries to give back the stocking, but at this point Booth feels that he is being patronized—"Only so long I can stand that little brother shit" (107)—and tells Lincoln to cut it open.

For Booth, the violation seems to come not just in having lost the card game, but in his brother's insistence on desanctifying what has become for him a sacred object. In an act of blind fury about all that has happened, he grabs Lincoln and shoots him; the stage directions say that Lincoln "slumps forward" (108) in a horrible imitation of the pretended death he has "rehearsed" every time he was assassinated as part of his job. Booth's monologue immediately after shooting Lincoln is revelatory:

> Think you can take my shit? My shit? That shit was mines. I kept it. Saved it. All this while. Through thick and through thin. Through fucking thick and through fucking thin, motherfucker. And you just gonna come up in here and mock my shit and call me two lefthanded talking bout how she coulda been jiving me then go steal from me? My *inheritance*. You stole my *inheritance*, man. That aint right. That aint right and you know it. (109)

The image of losing one's "inheritance" is a powerful one, again hearkening back to *Last Black Man*, because it evokes African-Americans' being stripped of that which they are owed after the long tragedy of slavery. In another historical sense, Parks also plays on the tragedy of inevitability by implying that "Booth" is destined to assassinate "Lincoln," that this is a fiercely ironic act of repetition (and one that again brings up the performative issue since the real Abraham Lincoln was shot by John Wilkes Booth while Lincoln was attending a play). As Michael Feingold suggests in his review of *Venus*, "Iconic moments of history, like Lincoln's assassination, became the nightmare from which black America was trying to escape" (81). In *Topdog*, Lincoln's job in which he is "assassinated" by tourists over and over thus becomes an eerie rehearsal for his own real death. Yet his own earlier words voice an awareness of the difference between the neatly packaged historical re-creation that the tourists want, and the messiness that actual murder entails. He tells Booth, "People are funny about they Lincoln shit. Its historical. People like they historical shit in a certain way. They like it to unfold the way they folded it up. Neatly like a book. Not raggedy and bloody and screaming" (50). As in *The America Play*, Parks seems to be fascinated with the distinction between history as narrative and history as experience, between the enforced neatness of text and the "raggedy" parts of the past that have been suppressed.

Finally, issues of commodification—the "selling" and exploitation of the black body—that were raised in such earlier plays as *Venus* are again brought to the forefront in *Topdog/Underdog*. Lincoln and Booth live in a culture in which what one has defines what one is. Lincoln's job impersonating Abraham Lincoln in a sense resembles the situation of the Venus Hottentot. In both cases, the capitalist exploiter makes money from the display and appropriation of a body, and audiences pay for the frisson of viewing and interacting with that body. Earlier, Lincoln tells Booth the story of how he successfully conned a little boy on the bus out of twenty dollars by promising his autograph for ten dollars (the boy, a victim of celebrity culture, confuses Lincoln in his costume with the famous figure he has studied in school) and by claiming that he'll bring back the change the next day. Booth longs for the trappings of luxury and success (as in the scene when he boosts the two full dress suits for himself and Lincoln), thinking that these will be key to his achieving happiness with Grace. He has been so deeply conditioned to believe that successful hustling is the key to fulfillment that he has lost all sight of what other human emotions are also involved, and Booth's subsequent shooting of Lincoln evolves from the sense that on every front, his ability to *perform*—as a man, as a successful capitalist-hustler-moneymaker, as a younger brother able to gain his older brother's respect—has been threatened because he feels himself to be acted upon rather than an actor. "Think you can take my shit?" he asks, after he has already shot Lincoln (109). His last, desperate moment of violence against his brother plays out his role as tragic hero, and the play ends with him holding Lincoln in his arms, crying with a primal "AAAAAAAAAAAAAAAAAAAH!" (109).

The ending is reminiscent of classical tragedy, and therefore risks accusations of obviousness. The critic writing in *USA Today* complains that "any fifth-grade English student could guess how the story ends before the first scene is over" (3d). Pochoda admonishes us, "We know, given their names, how they will end up. This is not the point. The game is the point" (36). Oddly, Robert Brustein, reviewing the play in *The New Republic,* believed that the play's "climax . . . does not seem sufficiently prepared for or realistically motivated," but mentions that it calls to mind not just the historical Booth and Lincoln, but also Cain and Abel (25–26). Brustein mentions that although he voted for the play for the Pulitzer, he sees it as "far from Parks's most ambitious writing" (25). Though otherwise deeply admiring of the play, Margo Jefferson writes in the *New York Times,* "When I say the ending was strong but disappointing I mean that, for me, it didn't fully live out the complexity of what had gone before" (22). But it is crucial to realize that this closing moment is overlaid with an awareness of the threatened black male body in American culture (Chaudhuri points out "the simple fact that these brothers are also *brothers*—African American men" [290]), and a heavily ironic playing out of the "inevitability" of Booth assassinating Lincoln (an event that seems to have been scripted for these characters beginning with their names at birth). *Venus* ends with the main character, who has already died a scene earlier, asking the audience to remember her, cutting her off in midsentence with "*Kiss* me *Kiss* me *Kiss* me *Kiss*" (162). Parks closes *Topdog* not with the freeze-frame of the brothers still in struggle (as Sam Shepard does in *True West*), but with the more brutal and powerful image of the aftermath of historical violence.

The "Red Letter" Plays
In the Blood and *Fucking A*

> I, Hester, am a red house lost in the thickening mist. One of my
> sides is clearly visible. The red one. The other side is hazy. I'm
> not sure if it's real.
>
> —Kathy Acker

> In *Fucking A*, Hester Smith and her world are foreign to us, but
> when we meet her, she draws us like a magnet, and we learn a
> lot about our own world. The same for Hester La Negrita in *In
> the Blood*. If there is a great psychic distance to travel between
> an audience member's seat and the character on stage—and if
> the character is very rich when you meet her—then the trip is
> incredibly intense, very visceral.
>
> —Suzan-Lori Parks (Sova 32)

In Kathy Acker's landmark novel *Blood and Guts in High School*,
first published in 1987, the heroine, Janey, rewrites herself as
Nathaniel Hawthorne's Hester Prynne from *The Scarlet Letter*, a text
she has been assigned to write about for a book report. Her "book
report" brilliantly mixes the clichés of the genre with her strong
identification with Hester as a social reject, mixed with Acker's own
commentary about commercialism; Janey writes, "All of them even
the hippies hated Hester Prynne because she was a freak and because

she couldn't be anything else and because she wouldn't be quiet and hide her freakiness like a bloody Kotex and because she was as wild and as insane as they come" (65). In the early 1990s, playwright Phyllis Nagy's adaptation of *The Scarlet Letter* also encouraged audiences to see Hester through the lens of contemporary feminism.

No postmodern artist, though, has taken on quite the same creative remapping of *The Scarlet Letter* as Suzan-Lori Parks does in her pair of "red letter" plays, *In the Blood* and *Fucking A*. Hester of *In the Blood* (a somewhat more naturalistic play) is a "welfare mother" attempting to raise her children and is continually exploited by characters like Welfare and the Doctor who claim to be helping her. In *Fucking A*, which includes both Brechtian-style songs and moments of an invented language called TALK, Hester earns her meager living as an abortionist in a dystopian, sci-fi society, and is trying desperately to see her jailed son, Monster, again.

Although the two pieces have been published together, they are normally performed separately. In fact, Parks says that *In the Blood* came to her "[i]n the middle of writing *Fucking A*" (Sova 32) and insists that Hester is an entirely separate character in each play. *In the Blood* premiered at the Papp Public Theater in New York in November 1999 (directed by David Esbjornson), and featured Charlayne Woodard as Hester; *Fucking A* received its premiere a few months later (in February 2000) at the experimental company Diverse Works / Infernal Bridegroom Productions in Houston, and starred Tamarie Cooper as Hester Smith in a production that Parks herself directed in collaboration with the company. The Public Theater production opened on March 16, 2003, and included S. Epatha Merkerson as Hester, Mos Def as Monster, and Daphne Rubin Vega as Canary Mary. Shawn-Marie Garrett writes that *Fucking A*, which was originally "a huge operatic work with 52 scenes and a parade of floats, among other extravagances," came originally out of "the foundation of *Venus*," whereas *In the Blood* happened when Parks "sat down" with one of the original versions of Hester, who suggested she belonged in a different play (134).

As the discussions in previous chapters have shown, Parks's works share an interest in digging back into the "holes" of history to resurrect bodies, especially black bodies, that have been commodified and exploited. We might recall her comment from the essay "Possession," quoted more fully in the introduction, that she sees theater as the place to "locate the ancestral burial ground, dig for bones, find bones, hear the bones sing, write it down" (4).

Parks's revisionist approaches to these historical moments and figures have used her unconventional theater style to get the audience to examine its own guilty spectatorship and cultural tourism, as we have seen, for example, in the intermission sequence of *Venus*. In her red- letter plays, Parks keeps her focus on cultural history, but the shift toward Hawthorne marks a recent movement in her work toward critique of the canon, in the same sense that her novel *Getting Mother's Body* (discussed in the final chapter) is a critical rewriting of another literary classic, William Faulkner's *As I Lay Dying*. In both *In the Blood* and *Fucking A*, Parks creates playful interactions with and against Hawthorne's Hester, in pursuit of a topic that deeply interested Hawthorne himself: the attempts of the self-regulating, theocratic society (the Puritans, but as Parks shows, contemporary society as well) to contain and devalue"otherness." Just as Acker's Janey is drawn to Hester because she is a "wild woman" (66) who has been marginalized by her society, Parks's two Hesters face the challenges of living in worlds that view them with fear and suspicion.

As most literature students know, Hawthorne's Hester is marked with a scarlet *A* and designated an outcast. Parks's Hesters, too, are shunned and marked by their race, class, and gender. In both of her plays, Hester is an African-American woman. Images of "otherness" in Hawthorne's novel are echoed in multiple references to the "Black Man" who is said to haunt the forest (and with whom the witches, like Mistress Hibbins, are said to consort), as well as the Indians, from whom it is said that Roger Chillingsworth learned his medicinal secrets. Hawthorne says of Hester that her years of being shunned have made her like a "wild Indian": "For years past she had looked from his estranged point of view at human institutions, and whatever priests or legislators had established; criticizing all with hardly more reverence than the Indian would feel for the clerical hand, the judicial robe, the pillory, the gallows, the fireside, or the church" (193). On the one hand, the novel evokes sympathy for the Indian by means of this link to Hester. On the other hand, Hawthorne's language here creates an ambiguity that deprives the Indian of political power: "[I]t serves to empty the 'savages' of their own history so as to universalize them as metaphors for Hester's development" (Bercovitch 29).

Hawthorne's Hester lives in a society that rejects her, but nevertheless finds its use for her: not only as the image of taboo behavior against which they can measure their own, but as a seamstress so skilled that the community leaders call upon her to embroider their robes. As Lauren Berlant points out, "Since Hester is seamstress to the collectivity, in her work she reweaves and reinforces the world as it already is, even as she is isolated from it and judged by it" (71). Parks uses her two plays to respond in two different ways. *In the Blood* begins (and ends) with a choral recitation that resembles Hawthorne's opening, in which the citizens of the town stare at Hester Prynne as she is exhibited upon a scaffold wearing her scarlet *A;* here, the Chorus comments on Hester La Negrita's behavior with such lines as "THERE SHE IS! / WHO DOES SHE THINK /SHE IS /THE NERVE SOME PEOPLE HAVE" (5).

This Hester attempts to sew but has problems even threading a needle; her difficulty at sustaining herself and her children involves regular interviews with a character named Welfare, who perpetrates acts of oppression upon her, asking her during their interview whether her hands are clean and then making her wash them again. When Welfare hands her the fabric to be sewn, she admonishes, "Make sure you don't get it dirty" (59). Hester sees the fabric as a ticket to a better life, and she speaks a monologue in which she fantasizes about the cloth: "Lets see what we making. Oooooh. Uh evening dress. Go to a party in. Drink champagne and shit" (62). Welfare, despite identifying herself as "a black woman too just like you" (60), is a version of Hawthorne's Puritan society that claims to be taking care of Hester Prynne yet keeps her in her place. Welfare blames Hester for not appreciating what she is given; her admonition is like a textbook of accusations about the behavior of women on welfare, a classic case of "blaming the victim":

We at Welfare are at the end of our rope with you. We put you in a job
and you quit. We put you in a shelter and you walk. We put you in
school and you drop out. Yr children are also truant. Word is they
steal. Stealing is a gateway crime, Hester. Perhaps your young daughter is pregnant. Who knows. We build bridges you burn them. We sew
safety nets, rub harder, good strong safety nets and you slip through
the weave. (54)

Welfare's imagery is reductive and objectifying, beginning with a
rope (which connotes capturing or even lynching), and ending with a
net (as if she were an animal to be trapped). Yvette Louis's comments
about prevalent attitudes toward unmarried black "welfare mothers"
apply to Hester's treatment:

In the aftermath of Moynihan's [1965] report, public discourses have
often pathologized the African American community as an underclass and the black woman as responsible for its alleged failings. The
recent political preoccupation with welfare reform and unwed motherhood, for instance, has "given a 'Black face' to welfare that has
made it easier for conservatives to blame African American families
than to go to the socioeconomic roots of poverty." (144; quoting
Cedric Herring, *African Americans and the Public Agenda* 20)

One need not go so far as David Yaffe in his review of the play in *The
Nation*, which sees the drama as a response to Bill Clinton's "politically motivated move to 'end welfare as we know it'" and says that
Parks's version of Hester "could be a propaganda piece for defenders
or opponents of the welfare state" (32). But Parks, whose motives
(and political views) in the play reveal a complex and sophisticated
understanding of her character's environment and predicament,
extends its social critique by having Reverend D say that "the poor"
aren't interesting unless they have been exoticized, even turned into
products of colonialism:

I want my poor looking good. I want my poor to know that it was me
who bought the such and such. I want my poor on tv. . . And I dont
want local poor. Local poor dont look good. Gimmie foreign poor.
Poverty exotica. (73)

Indeed, Hawthorne refers to the self-interest involved in overseeing the fate of outsiders like Hester Prynne; he comments that although it may seem surprising to have the governor take an interest in Hester, "matters of even slighter public interest, and of far less intrinsic weight than the welfare of Hester and her child, were strangely mixed up with the deliberations of legislators and acts of state" (95).

In the Blood's structure includes a series of "confessions" from various characters—the Doctor, Welfare, Amiga Gringa, Reverend D, Chilli—who speak directly to the audience. Parks tells interviewer Kathy Sova, "I use the confessions, the characters' interior monologues, to describe events that happened offstage. As we hear confession after confession, it occurs to us that so much is happening offstage that we must ask, 'What is going to happen in front of us?'" (Sova 32). These confessions make clear that all of these characters have profited from sexual exploitation of Hester. Amiga Gringa, for instance, says, "It took a little cajoling to get her to do it with me / for an invited audience. / For a dime a look. / Over at my place" (72). The Doctor rhapsodizes that "she gave herself to me in a way that I had never experienced even with women Ive paid" (44). Even Welfare, while insisting upon the "well-drawn boundary line" (62) between herself and her clients, tells a story about her and her husband using Hester together for their sexual gratification (which shows the subtext of her earlier attempt to correct Hester's behavior when she reminded her of "that afternoon with the teacups" [57]). In the Know Theatre Tribe production in May 2006, directed by Jason Bruffy, for each "confession" the audience was shown abstract film footage of Hester and the speaking character in sexualized poses. This made the spectators complicit in the voyeuristic, exploitative appropriation of Hester's image (Parks, as we have seen, frequently uses competing film footage within her plays). But it perhaps obscured the idea that each speaker performs a sort of testimony that may be sensationalized in and of itself. That is, unless we see each film sequence as a projection of what is inside the speaker's head, the footage may grant too much credibility to the speakers instead of letting the audience wonder how much they are embroidering their stories.

Embrya deShango in *In the Blood,* director Jason Bruffy. Know Theatre of Cincinnati. Photo by Deogracias Lerma.

In *Fucking A,* Hester works as an abortionist (which is what the *A* on her chest stands for). Again, she is both an outcast and a necessary component of her society; as her friend Canary Mary the prostitute says to her, "No one would wanna kill you. We need you too much. Like me, you perform one of those disrespectable but most necessary services" (121). To a certain degree, Hester (in this very Brechtian play) is like Brecht's Mother Courage, pursuing her job with relentless effort and causing the audience to question her society rather than questioning it herself. The *USA Today* review of the Public Theater production praises S. Epatha Merkerson's performance for bringing out these qualities in Hester:

> It's a mesmerizing spectacle, bringing to mind such disturbed figures as Sweeney Todd and Medea. Parks's character, Hester Smith, has gotten a raw deal from life and is determined to avenge herself, even if it means sealing her own destruction. . . . There is much emphasis on maternal yearning and class bias, much talk of angels and monsters, and how society can turn the former into the latter. . . . Merkerson absorbs her character's tough, tender and tortured qualities so convincingly that we never question this loving mom's conviction, even when her choices become horrific. ("Another Hester" 4D)

Hester's clashes with the Freedom Fund character in this play resemble Hester La Negrita's conflicts with Welfare in *In the Blood*; although Freedom Fund says she admires Hester for working hard at her job, she doesn't believe Hester's insistence on her jailed son's honesty and claims that he is a "hardened criminal" (134). In both cases, these figures claim to know what is best for Hester, yet deprive her of the right to make her own choices. Parks adds a further sardonic comment in *Fucking A* by following the Butcher's wild monologue (an extravagant set piece that is sometimes, sadly, cut from production) about the extreme behaviors of his daughter Lulu with the remark, "Shes not eligible for the Freedom Fund program" (161).

Another component of identity and social class for all three Hesters is the issue of reading, literacy, and textuality. Of course, in Hawthorne's novel, "reading" the scarlet *A* is a central theme; the role of reading also figures prominently in Hester Prynne's interactions with her daughter Pearl. Even though Pearl in *The Scarlet Letter* is the product of Hester's "sin," she is also her treasure, as her name itself attests. Pearl herself is difficult to "read" because she is so defiantly unlike other children in the community, and is more an elf or a sprite than a child. Hawthorne writes that "in this one child there were many children, comprehending the full scope between the wild-flower prettiness of a peasant-baby, and the pomp, in little, of an infant princess" (85). In *Blood and Guts,* Janey writes in her book report that Pearl is "as wild as they come. *Wild* in the Puritan New England Society Hawthorne writes about means *evil anti-society criminal*" (93). She goes on to say that the men in the town "want to keep the child so they can train the child to suck their cocks. That's what's known as education" (94).

Parks literalizes the "many children" within Pearl by giving Hester La Negrita five of them: Jabber, Baby, Bully, Trouble, and Beauty. In Hawthorne's novel, it is through the act of reading—of peeking into Reverend Dimmesdale's private notes when he is asleep—that Chillingsworth confirms Dimmesdale's identity as Pearl's secret father. "TEACH ME A NEW LANGUAGE, DIMWIT [Dimmesdale]," writes Acker's Janey. "A LANGUAGE THAT MEANS SOMETHING TO ME" (96). In both red-letter plays, Parks emphasizes the illiteracy of the two Hesters—*In the Blood,* for instance, begins with Hester scrutinizing the word "Slut" written in graffiti on the wall under the bridge where they live, and asking her oldest son Jabber whether it is a "good word or a bad word" (9). Initially, Jabber refuses to answer, leading to the pivotal later moment of the play in which she beats him to death. It is crucial to understand, though, that this Hester has a gifted imagination; she helps her children to enjoy the meager soup that she feeds them for dinner by telling them that it has everything they love in it—"Theres carrots in there. Theres meat. Theres oranges. Theres pie" (17), and her bedtime story for them seems to be a fairy tale created as an imaginative retelling of the children's five fathers. She attempts to end the story by saying, "And they was all happy," but Jabber insists that there must be "bad news" still to come: "Theres always bad news" (20). Robert Brustein, otherwise a supporter of Parks's work, derides the Public Theater production as "one of those inspirational pieces about the Human Capacity to Prevail and Endure, animated more by the energies of victimology than by Parks's customary poetic resources" ("The Element of Surprise" 31, 32). Brustein, however, misses the tragic clash between Hester's attempts to "Prevail and Endure," and the myriad forces of society that work against her.

In the world of *Fucking A*, few in the underclass know how to write, and those who need to do so hire a Scribe; when at one point the Scribe attempts to leave his shop, the Butcher admonishes him, "Theres lots of people want writing done and yr shops closed. That's bad business" (140). Hester has Canary read her her son's letter from prison, and uses the Scribe to write back; she tells the Butcher, "He makes the nicest looking letters. Even when he's sloshed. Such pretty shapes, straight bold lines and gentle curls. Makes me wish I could read. And write too" (159). Interestingly, the Scribe himself bears a relation to Hester in his description of the scars he received from being beaten by his father: "Dad wanted me to make something of myself. So he stood over me with a stick. I still got the welts, well, the scars of the welts. . . . Perfectly formed letters at 3 years old. The most beautiful alphabet you've ever seen" (140).

Parks's focus on illiteracy, as well as on the struggle to transcend one's social class by learning to read, is also crucial to Maria Irene Fornes's dramas, such as *Mud* and *The Conduct of Life*. Like Fornes, Parks is interested in the historical sense in which women have been kept in their place by being denied the right to literacy; the image has further resonance if we consider that African-American slaves were also denied access to forms of education that could lead to their rebellion. Discussing how literacy helped him realize that he could work toward ending his enslavement, Frederick Douglass comments, "[I]t is almost an unpardonable offence to teach slaves to read in this Christian country" (52). Similarly, in *Our Nig*, Harriet E. Wilson writes of Mrs. Bellmont (one of the antagonists) that she "was in doubt about the utility of attempting to educate people of color, who were incapable of elevation" (30).

Parks explores the issues of readability and language in *Fucking A* by giving the characters an alternative dialect, called TALK, which they use most often when the women are discussing biological and sexual behavior. TALK is primarily a language for females; in a late scene, the Second Hunter seems to be embarrassed after the First Hunter hears him using TALK with Hester. The First Hunter tells him, "My wife wants me to learn it but I say no way. Keep that stuff private. Like it should be. Thats what I say" (146). TALK is amusing to read or hear because it draws upon unfamiliar combinations of familiar sounds; "abortion," for instance, is an "Abah-nazip." Much like Tom Stoppard and David Ives, Parks plays with the audience's need to "decode" the drama. Her opening stage directions say that the production should provide a "nonaudible simultaneous English translation" (115); this can be interpreted as tongue-in-cheek suggestion, or perhaps as a desire to have the language work subconsciously on the minds of the spectators, much as we are inadvertently drawn into the anatomical vocabulary in *Venus.* In the Public Theater production, supertitles (which were also used, in Brechtian fashion, to announce the songs) displayed English translations of TALK. At the same time, Parks hearkens back to the creation of coded and alternative languages in historical African-American culture (and reminds us of such coded languages that exist in contemporary cultural groups, including "women's" languages). The difficulty of "reading" or appropriating the characters is thus thrown back to us, much as Hawthorne's Hester is never fully "readable" by the people of the town or by the consumers of his text.

In Hawthorne's *Scarlet Letter,* Hester is betrayed by both of the men in her life. Roger Chillingsworth, her former husband who reappears in the town as a physician but does not reveal his identity, uses his power—and his knowledge of Hester's partner in guilt—to manipulate both Hester and this partner, Reverend Dimmesdale. Dimmesdale, too, is an instrument of torture because of his refusal to admit publicly that he is the father of Hester's child. Dimmesdale is in some ways a sympathetic character because he is plagued by feelings of self-recrimination; even Acker's Janey writes in her book report, "Like Hester, Dimwit [Dimmesdale] hates himself. Like Hester, Dimwit is conscious he doesn't understand what's happening. Hester sees Dimwit's going crazy and in deepening torture" (98). In

Hawthorne's novel, he is also a coward in his inability to step forward and claim responsibility for Hester's public torture and rejection. Chillingsworth and Dimmesdale are figured fairly obviously in *In the Blood* as Chilli and Reverend D (as well as the Doctor, who persuades her to get sterilized or "spayed" so that she'll be "[c]lean as a whistle" [85]), and in rather different ways as the Butcher and the Monster (her son) in *Fucking A*. Chilli initially reapproaches Hester because he has had a romanticized view of her as the suffering mother—"I carried around this picture of you. Sad and lonely with our child on yr hip" (96)—but flees when he realizes that the reality is rather different. In his "confession" speech immediately afterward, he admits, "She was my first. / We was young. / Times change" (98). Reverend D initially promises Hester that he will take up a collection for her at his church, but eventually he rejects her, saying, "Don't ever come back here again! Ever! Yll never get nothing from me! Common Slut. Tell on me! Go on! Tell the world! I'll crush you underfoot"(103). We can see Reverend D's real motives in his confession speech, aptly titled, "Suffering is an Enormous Turn- On" (78). Parks is less willing than Hawthorne to offer sympathy for the Reverend; her character is an implicit critique of the ambiguous feelings we have for Dimmesdale when he dies at the end of the novel.

Fucking A initially sets up a more promising relationship for Hester in her friendship with the Butcher. One form of betrayal, though, comes when Jailbait—the wrong prisoner—arrives for the picnic and Hester, not recognizing him, assumes that he is her long-unseen son; the sequence culminates in Jailbait telling Hester that her real son is dead, then raping her while she is "struck dumb with grief and disbelief" (184). When her son Monster shows up at Hester's house, he in turn pretends to be another former fellow inmate of her "dead" son, and Hester is initially skeptical even when he shows her the scar with which she marked him as a child ("When they comed to take him away, just before they took him, I bit him. Hard . . . He'll always have my mark" [166]). Like *In the Blood*, though, the play ends in a Medean moment when Hester finally acknowledges Monster's identity, but kills him before he is caught by the Hunters. This sacrifice again evokes Parks's reflections in "Possession" about African-

Embrya deShango and Martin Andrews in *In the Blood*, director Jason Bruffy. Know Theatre of Cincinnati. Photo by Deogracias Lerma.

American history and "ancestral burial grounds"—particularly when the burial grounds themselves do not even exist as places for commemoration. In this case, Hester's decision to "save" Monster by killing him herself conjures up slave narratives in which the mother chooses to end the child's life rather than give the child up to slavery. The Sethe–Margaret Garner story in Toni Morrison's *Beloved* draws upon this legacy (see Moglen 205–6 for a discussion of *Beloved*'s sources). Barbara Christian's words about Morrison's novel shed some light upon Parks's debt to Morrison:

> In *Beloved*, Morrison not only explores the psychic horror of those who can no longer call their ancestors' names but also the dilemma of the mother who knows her children will be born into and live in the realm of those who cannot call their ancestors' names. Sethe's killing of her already-crawling baby is not only the killing of that individual baby but also the collective anguish African-American women must have experienced when they realized their children were cut off forever from their "living dead," who would never be called upon, remembered, or fed. (369)

Finally, there is the question of the scarlet *A* itself that Hawthorne's Hester is forced to wear when she is branded an adulteress. The letter becomes so much a part of her that when she casts it off into a creek, Pearl refuses to recognize her until she puts it back on. While critics have speculated endlessly about the meanings of the *A*, they return repeatedly to it as a marker that creates both an identity for and an identification with the heroine. In this sense, Rita K. Gollin remarks, one of the many associations of the *A* is with Hawthorne himself as *"Artist* or even *Author"*; she adds that the novel "can be approached as a network of statements about vocations chosen, evaded, and changed" (180). Berlant adds that while "[a]t first transfigured by the letter's power as the law's sign, Hester turns the 'A' into her own monogram" (142).

In the Blood makes the *A* the only letter that Hester knows how to write. For her, too, it has become a kind of bodily marking, as we see when Jabber reminds her of its shape: "Legs apart hands crost the chest like I showed you," he tells her (11). After she kills Jabber, she writes an *A* on the ground in his blood: "Looks good Jabber, dont it? Dont it, huh?" (106). The *A* for Hester becomes conflated with the "hand of fate" (77, 84) that she has envisioned coming down toward her throughout the play: it is the writing on the wall, like the word "slut" that we see in grafitti at the beginning, but it is also the mark of the judgment against her, as others find the *A* on the ground and attempt to decipher its meaning after Hester has been arrested for the murder. "First letter of the alphabet," remarks the Doctor. "That's as far as she got," Welfare responds (109).

In *Fucking A*, the letter marks her as an abortionist; we are told that this is the law, and so although she prefers to cover the "A," she wears it:

> The brand comes with the job is all I know. "And the brand must be visible at all times." Thats the law. Everyone knows what I do— but then, my A is also like a shingle and a license, so nobodyll ever get suckered by a charlatan.
> *(Rest)*
> What we do is bad. And good. And bad and good and good and bad. Theres no easy way to look at it.

(Rest)
Go to prison or take this job. That was my choice. Choose A or
choose B. I chose A. (164–65)

Hester has chosen A, even though the branding or literalizing of her choice appears to be repulsive to others; at one point, one of the Hunters tries to get her to cover it up. Reflected in the imagery of Hester's bloody apron and tools (214–15), the letter "weeps" continuously "as a fresh wound would" (125), and she remarks, "The A looks so fresh, like they branded me yesterday" (125).

Rendering the *A* as a bodily mark reflects Janey's sense in Acker's novel that the treatment of Hester becomes inseparable from her physical sense of self: "At this point in *The Scarlet Letter* and in my life politics don't disappear but take place inside my body" (97). In *Fucking A*, the branding image invokes slavery (as well as Nazism), and it allows Parks to create a disturbing sense of what it means for the black female body to be controlled and manipulated. Again, this recalls the image of Saartjie Baartman in *Venus*—but in rewriting Hester Prynne, Parks takes another character (this time an American one) who has been famously romanticized and mystified, and insists that we consider her again through the lens of our cruel and continuing histories of oppression.

365 *Plays,* "New Black Math," and Other Media

> WOMAN. Youve made a career of it. Hole digging.
> MAN. Thats the kicker. You think one would satisfy. Wrong.
> Digging holes creates the need to dig holes.
>
> — *Hole* (365 *Days/*365 *Plays* 30)

Parks's nontheatrical creations have, ever since the beginning of her career, crossed into other genres ranging from fiction to film to songwriting. While the discussions that follow do not attempt to provide comprehensive analyses of these varied and exciting projects—since the focus of this study is her career for the stage—they should provide a sense of the extraordinary range of her work, as well as the themes and styles that resonate even in other media. The last section of this chapter discusses Parks's most recent dramatic projects, including her ambitious 365 *Days/*365 *Plays.*

Getting Mother's Body

In 2003, Random House published Parks's first novel, *Getting Mother's Body* (though she says that she had been writing novels since the age of five), which she completed at the same time that *Topdog/Underdog* was getting media attention. The novel concerns the family and acquaintances of a young African-American woman in rural Texas, Billy Beede, whose dead mother Willa Mae's jewels are supposedly buried with her and who becomes the object of a journey to dig her up. Parks had long been inspired by William Faulkner, and the debt that the book owes to his *As I Lay Dying* is obvious, from the subject (the tragicomic idea of exposing all of the characters' separate and secret motives for getting to the body of the dead mother) to the style of creating the chapters as interior monologues in the voices of the various characters. Yet this is also very much an original story, grounded in issues of race, gender, place, history, and social class, that takes up many of Parks's favorite themes.

Parks tells interviewer Vicki Curry about why she chose to do this project as a novel:

> I knew it wasn't a play, you know, because it's about place. It's very much about landscape. It's very much about the interior thoughts of the characters, which you can get in a play from a soliloquy, but it's really not the same.

Yet the novel is clearly informed by her dramatic sensibility: the mother, Willa (she is dead, but has monologues throughout) was a singer and an adept performer of con games (and as a child, other kids paid to watch her roll in a barrel down a hill). The dialogue ricochets with the rhythm, panache, and physical attention to sound that Parks's plays have. Homer speaks about their situation as if they were like Parks's "figures" (almost as if the author were questioning whether the novel was going in this direction): "The Negro-College-Going Youth eyeballing the White- Just-Back-From-Fishing Sheriff. If we was in a play those would be our parts" (167).

But this is indeed a novel about place, and about race and history as well. Its setting is Texas (one of the states where Parks lived as a child during her father's military career), and the name of the town where it begins should sound familiar to readers of her plays: Lincoln. It takes place in 1963, before the Kennedy assassination and in the early years of the civil rights movement, which is alluded to several times, as these characters live under the racism of their period and location. The white bus driver is suspicious about letting Billy onto his bus, saying, "I don't want no Freedom Riders, now" (56), and her Uncle Teddy (named for Teddy Roosevelt) tells her to sit in the back. At one point, Dill's friend Little Walter tries to persuade his pastor to join him at the March on Washington, where Martin Luther King will be speaking; when the pastor refuses, Little Walter says it's because he's "sour cause you ain't been asked to speak" (87). When Billy steals Dill's truck, Dill's initial reaction is that it must have been a bunch of white boys who would be thinking, "It's just a nigger's truck. A nigger who's doing well for herself. A bulldagger nigger who got a sow with thirteen new nigger-sow piglets" (140). When Homer and Roosevelt (Teddy) get thrown into jail by a racist sheriff, we hear quite a bit of the sheriff's hateful talk, including his words to Homer as Homer sits still: "You look like Martin Luther Coon. . . . That'd be a good-looking feather in my cap" (167). Parks portrays characters who live under oppressive circumstances that they almost take for granted; she illustrates a time and place in which change is on the horizon, where the characters are suspended in a moment when their lives are undervalued. Roosevelt's words reflect the issue of slavery and its inheritance that we saw in Parks's two Lincoln plays:

> At least Billy won't be traveling alone. It ain't safe out there for a Negro gal. It's 1963 and a Negro life is cheap. The life of a Negro man is cheap. The life of a Negro woman is cheaper. The price of everything is always going up though, so could be that the price of a Negro life too will get high. Maybe the price'll rise to reach the value of the cost we brought in slavery times. Not this year though. Not the next. Maybe by nineteen hundred and seventy. Maybe by nineteen hundred and eighty or nineteen hundred and ninety the price will go up. Maybe by the year two thousand, but surely, the world will end by then. (124)

Central to the novel is the presence of the dead mother, Willa Mae, a blues singer and extravagant sexual presence whose character owes something to Alice Walker's Shug in *The Color Purple*, even down to her bisexuality (Willa names her daughter after Billie Holiday). (The one-legged mother substitute, Aunt June, also owes something to Eva Peace in Toni Morrison's *Sula*.) One of the wonderful surprises in Faulkner's *As I Lay Dying* comes when, in the middle of the novel, we get a monologue from the dead mother Addie Bundren, who reveals her secret adulterous past and her hatred for her family. Parks, too, allows the dead mother to speak—one of several examples of resurrection in the novel, as will be discussed shortly—but even more prolifically, as she has monologues throughout the book. Most of Willa's chapters are in the form of blues songs, a form to which Parks has been increasingly drawn in her plays (see discussion in the introduction) and that coincides with her marriage to blues musician Paul Oscher at the time she was writing this book. Parks tells Curry that she included songs in the novel "because there are parts in the characters' lives where regular language will not express what they're feeling," and when she has performed parts of the book on lecture tours, Parks has played and sung some of these songs on the guitar herself and has recorded them on a CD.

What is interesting about Willa's songs is that the earliest ones in the novel, such as "Big Hole Blues" (30) or "Willa Mae's Blues" (66), follow the conventional blues structure of repetition and variation with signifying twists in the closing line of each stanza (in the last line of each verse of "Willa Mae's Blues," for example, the wife who finds out that the singer is the "other woman" takes an additional step of revenge). As her songs continue, they take on additional overtones of betrayal and violence as the patterns are disrupted (see "Hatchet Tree Blues," 142), echo the mournfulness of spirituals (see the untitled song with the refrain "ain't I gone," 157), or speak of imprisonment (see the song that concludes, "Guess I'll live in this great prison till I die," 176), or death ("It's a cold cold lonesome hole," 218). At moments, Willa's voice breaks free from the songs and she has a brief interior monologue that exists in a limbo beyond the grave, such as when she explains how to do a con game called the "ring trick" and casts its various roles (199). As a kind of absent presence, Willa directs the action of the novel and pervades the memories of every character who knew her, from her lover Dill to her daughter Billy. She is re-membered through her songs, but also has some agency as a narrator figure (such as when she speaks about her relationship with Dill, 225). Indeed, at one point she interrupts her song about naming called "Promise Land" and gives a list of Old Daddy Beede's and Willameena Drummer's sixteen children, all named "after presidents and philanthropists . . . [and] after words they liked saying" (246). At the end of this sequence, she remembers seeing her daughter Billy walk behind her in the sand, "putting her feet prints where my feets had already made a mark. Good Lord, I thought, my child's following in my footsteps. But I tried not to worry. The way I see it, you can only dig a hole so deep" (247). Willa is caught between wanting to cast off her legacies (and she died from a self-induced abortion) and to be part of the act of re-membering.

One of Willa's legacies to Billy is the ability to recognize the "Hole" in someone, which she says everyone has: "Soft spot, sweet spot, opening, blind spot, Itch, Gap, call it what you want but I call it a Hole" (30–31). To figure out another person's Hole is to figure out what he or she is missing, or longs for, and to exploit that knowledge. To get Mrs. Jackson to lower the price on the wedding dress in her window, for example, Billy takes advantage of Mrs. Jackson's memory of her own wedding day and her sympathy that Billy has lost her mother. She says this is the first time she has been aware of how to use this knowledge: "Words shape theirselves in my mouth and I start talking without thinking of what I need to say. It's like The Hole shapes the words for me and I don't got to think or nothing" (27). The Hole is a place of creation (a womb) and intuition, but it also echoes the Great Hole of History in *The America Play:* it is a space within which a legacy is enacted, a space where history is passed on, significantly in this case from mother to daughter.

Finally, the tropes of digging and resurrection that are omnipresent in Parks's plays make significant appearances in this novel, whose plot after all is concerned with the digging up of the mother's body. Snipes, Billy's lover at the beginning of the novel (who runs back to his wife after discovering Billy is pregnant), is in the coffin business (the doctor wants to be buried in a coffin that looks like a doctor's bag), and the Jacksons run a funeral parlor, so the story from the outset revisits the interest in death and funerals that we see in

Last Black Man, Venus, and other stage works by Parks. The Jacksons' son is named Lazarus—"I was born not breathing," he explains, and in a sense he gets another life at the end of the novel when Billy finally agrees to marry him. And like the Foundling Father and his son Brazil in *The America Play,* Lazarus is a gravedigger; when the digging up of Willa happens, he offers an elaborate illustration of the proper procedure for unearthing a corpse: "There's a certain method to digging a grave," he says. "You don't just pop the spade to the dirt willy-nilly, there's a certain method to it" (250). Willa, it turns out, was buried with a secret: right when the other characters are dismayed to see that she is not wearing any of the expensive jewelry they had hoped to find (and Dill thinks she already got all of it for herself), Billy shows them the place in the hem of Willa's dress where her diamond ring was hidden. Thus, it is not just through her monologues but through the literal unburying of her corpse that Willa exerts control over the plot of the novel. Perhaps unlike Venus, though, she is ultimately laid back to rest. Strikingly, it is her daughter Billy who gets the last thoughts on the subject (and her lines rather interestingly echo the "we give birth astride of a grave" speech in Beckett's *Godot*): "When I seen her bones I knew what we all knew, that we's all gonna end up in a grave someday, but there's stops in between there and now" (257).

Screenwriting: *Girl 6, Their Eyes Were Watching God,* and Other Film Work

Girl 6

In 1990, Parks and Bruce Hainley made a short (thirty-five-minute) film, *Anemone Me,* which was shown at several shorts festivals, but it was not until the mid-1990s that she began to do some feature-length screenwriting, which has continued intermittently throughout her career. Her first major foray into film was as screenwriter for Spike Lee's 1996 feature *Girl 6.* Although the film seems more integral to Lee's oeuvre than Parks's, it evinces her trademark interests and style. (Lee's trademark slogan that accompanies his Forty Acres and a Mule insignia—"Ya Dig—Sho Nuff"—seems compatible with

Parks's playful but purposeful interests.) Parks says in the "Making of *Girl 6*" interview, "I wanted to write a very strong woman character, not just a victim . . . and I wanted it also to be funny . . . the fantasy element's very exciting."

Because the tone of the film is complicated, its genre was difficult to determine for purposes of marketing, and one couldn't tell whether the tag line of the trailer was tongue in cheek: "She's the only thing better than being there." It was initially advertised as a comedy, quoting the words "high-energy party" from Janet Maslin's *New York Times* review (C3), and its Prince soundtrack and star-studded cast (featuring, among others, small roles played by Madonna and Naomi Campbell) were strong selling points. Yet the film does not sit comfortably as a simple comedy because we glimpse the brutal, degrading (and even scary, when she is pursued by a caller) side of Girl 6's life. In his review of *In the Blood*, David Yaffe says that "we are drawn in to the title character's sensual life, only to be jolted by her masochistic victimization" (32). It is also quite striking to note that *Girl 6* was released in New York within the same month that *Venus* opened there at the Public Theater: the two works are worth comparing for their treatment of the central, exploited heroine.

Much like Saartjie, popularly known as only Venus (and no one knows her African name), the protagonist of this film (played by Theresa Randle) is known only as Girl 6 or by one of her pseudonyms, Lovely. She is delighted late in the film to be called "Judy" by her ex-husband, but we never know whether that's her real name. The film begins with a number of parodic jabs about show business, as director Quentin Tarantino, who had recently been on the receiving end of anger about his use of words like "nigger" in *Pulp Fiction*, plays a sleazy filmmaker who wants the protagonist to take her top off as part of the audition. (Maslin rightly points out in her review that "Mr. Lee might have better championed her dignity by not having her do the same for his own camera" [C3]). The director, "Q.T." (Tarantino in a sense is playing himself), tells her that he is doing "the greatest romantic African-American film ever made, directed by me, of course, from an African-American point of view." When he has her turn and rotate slowly for the camera, it is hard not to be reminded of Venus rotating for the spectators in that play: both works critique a black woman's being objectified for the purposes of entertainment and consumption (though the film's success in accomplishing this critique is questionable).

The issue of the black actress as commodity continues when we see the protagonist being screamed at by her acting coach, an older black woman, in a scene that parodies the worst excesses of histrionic actor training. "It needs a bottom—where's the bottom?" her coach demands. "Drop into the pain . . . turn it into something special." Our heroine tries to respond, but the acting coach is lost in her own narcissistic melodrama. It turns out that the coach, too, is driven by profit: "If you would pay me, you would show that you have respect for your art form." The film cuts to images of the protagonist handing out flyers for computer seminars and being told by a production assistant while she is working as an extra, "You can pee when I say you can pee." Parks and Lee are playing out the hypocrisy one encounters in attempting to follow one's "art" as an actor, which is why the central character succumbs to the promise of big bucks as another type of performer: one who works for a phone sex line.

This new workplace is portrayed as a kind of sisterhood with a matriarchal boss, Lil (who is reminiscent of the Mother-Showman in *Venus*, though not as malicious). The phone sex operators share training and swap anecdotes, and the office environment, with its cubicles and training seminars, looks like much of the corporate world; a phone sex worker calls herself "a telecommunications sales representative." There is a funny but disturbing sequence when Girl 6 receives a corsage and congratulations from her coworkers when she "pops her cherry"—that is, for the first time gets a caller to ejaculate. The phone sex training is a site for Parks and Lee to comment on performance and race. The workers are given a list of "types" for which they must be able to create characters (girl next door, transsexual, dominatrix, etc.), and our heroine describes hers, with her clear favorite being her girl next door, "Lovely." She channels her need to perform, to create, into these roles. At the same time, this world is racialized, as Lil tells the workers (most of whom are women of color) that unless a caller requests otherwise, "all of you girls are W-H-I-T-E" (she spells the word out on the whiteboard as she says it).

One clear theme of the film is fantasy and its link to both gender and performance. When Girl 6 and the others are at work, the callers want to play out domination fantasies. One man gets aroused by telling the heroine how he used one company to smash another; a different one has her pretend that she is a housewife scrubbing the floor: "I'm making slow soapy circles on the linoleum with my scrub brush," she says. "A woman's work is never done," the caller responds. In one parodic scene, a phone worker draws in her sketchbook while she excites her caller simply by listing the foods she can buy at the grocery store. Some of the callers need psychological counseling more than sex, such as Bob Regular from Tucson (with whom Girl 6 becomes obsessed), who calls about his mother dying of cancer. In a sequence that comments on the racial disparity between what we see and what the caller wants to hear, Girl 29, a black phone sex worker dressed like a punkette (green lipstick, black leather) tells her caller, "Don't I look pretty with my long blonde hair and my big blue eyes?" Like Venus, the phone workers profit from the laughably craven expectations of the callers—and do so with more than a hint of sarcasm and wisdom—yet they are complicit in this exploitation and subjects of (sexual) exploitation themselves.

Fantasy and performance are given another dimension in the film as we see the heroine change wigs and costumes to act out fantasias of her own, in which she portrays black female characters of the past. She becomes Dorothy Dandridge in *Carmen Jones*, saying, "I gotta be free." In another mock film sequence, she plays Foxy Brown and fights a roomful of thugs ("Talk to me fast, baby, I got five heavy tripping jive turkeys on my tail"); at the end of it, she flashes her ID badge, which says "Lovely Brown." As her job begins to take its toll, she enacts the sitcom *The Jeffersons*, where she is the daughter, and her father concludes the sequence by shooting the phone. When near the end of the film she is on her way to Los Angeles for a fresh start, she fantasizes that she is a movie star meeting a director in a forties glamour film as his obsequious (black female) assistant reassures her that the audition is "not a reading—he just wants to have a little meeting with you."

The men in Girl 6's real world are portrayed with striking ambiguity. Her neighbor Jimmy (played by Spike Lee) tries to persuade her that the phone sex career is not the achievement of her hopes: "How you actin?" he asks. "Is there a phone sex hall of fame?" But Jimmy, too, lives in a kind of fantasy world where he can't pay his rent but holds tightly on to his collection of rare baseball cards and sports memorabilia (he shows her his Ken Griffey Jr. card and calls it "better than stocks"). He seems to have evolved somewhat near the end when he tells Girl 6 that he has sold some of his cards, and gives her a 1964 (the year Parks was born) "Tops in NL" card signed by Hank Aaron and Willie Mays. The protagonist's ex-husband (played by Isaiah Washington) is also an ambiguous character. He has rejected the world of commerce entirely, stealing food for a living but taking—he tells her—only what he needs (we see the anger of Korean store owners as he flees with fruit in a baby carrier, and his verbal list of food parallels the earlier phone sex worker's list, so there is an implicit critique of his actions). Attempting to get back into his ex- wife's good graces, he gives her an old *Life* magazine with Dorothy Dandridge on the cover. A pivotal scene occurs when Girl 6—sitting across from him at a diner—acts out one of her phone calls, then becomes furious when he gets sexually excited. "I was just playing with you," she says, but to him there is no such distinction. The boundaries she draws between her performances and real life break down in disturbing ways as she begins moonlighting with another phone sex agency (whose head is played by Madonna) which has her take calls at home, and is pursued by a violent sadist who learns her address. In one of Lee's characteristically romantic visual moments (see, for example, the color sequence in *She's Gotta Have It* or the ending of *Mo Better Blues*), Girl 6 ("Judy") embraces her ex-husband just as she is about to leave for LA, and telephones drop out of the sky around them and smash on the ground. The romanticism may be Lee, but the surrealism of the sequence could easily be Parks.

One more thread from the "outside world" woven through the story is a news item with which Girl 6 becomes fascinated (tears roll down her cheeks when she hears the initial broadcast), about an eight-year-old black girl named Angela King who was playing in her Harlem building and fell down an elevator shaft. Updates report that she is in critical condition. Girl 6 identifies with the vulnerability of the little girl. "It started as a game," the reporter says, and we see the black dolls that our protagonist keeps in her apartment—and she envisions herself falling down an elevator shaft, an image of her fears. On the one hand, Girl 6's visit to the little girl at the end to give her a gift (presumably it's the baseball card that Jimmy gave her) seems to represent our heroine's efforts toward recovery. On the other hand—since with Parks such gestures are fraught with ambiguity, as in *Imperceptible Mutabilities*—we saw an earlier sequence in which Halle Berry was flaunting her celebrity visit to the little girl in the hospital, so we still have to wonder whether our heroine's behavior is also an unconscious acting out of her continuing fantasy of being (or behaving like) a movie star.

This ambiguity is reinforced by the end of the film, in which we see Girl 6 in LA, auditioning for another sleazy director (played by Ron Silver) who tells her to take her top off, in a parallel to the film's opening scene. She refuses and speaks into the camera, saying that enough is enough. Dropping her script on the floor on the way out, she pretends that doing so was a mistake ("Oops!") but the director is impressed with her verve. In the last shots, she walks across Dorothy Dandridge's star on the Walk of Fame and heads toward a marquee that announces *Girl 6*. But the self-referential gesture is never explained: is this another fantasy sequence? Is she now starring in a film about her own life story as a phone sex worker? Is this a metafilmic moment in which we the audience see her walking into the same film we have just been watching? Or could more than one of these be true? The cyclicity we have seen in many of Parks's works combines with Lee's predilection for seemingly upbeat endings that force the viewer to make choices (see the competing quotations from Malcolm X and Martin Luther King at the end of *Do the Right Thing*, for example). He asserts in the interview on "The Making of *Girl 6*" that our heroine is "triumphant" at the end: "Her feet are firmly planted on the ground." But the effect is more ambiguous than that, thanks in part to Parks. At the end of this film, Girl 6, like Venus, still longs for love and has achieved a certain kind of immortality, but we are left asking whether she was able to make choices—and what price she has paid along the way.

Their Eyes Were Watching God

Not all of the screenwriting projects that Parks has worked on have been filmed. These include several adaptations: Ruthie Bolton's novel *Gal* for Universal Pictures, and Toni Morrison's novel *Paradise* for Oprah Winfrey. She was also an uncredited writer (with Robert Eisele) for Denzel Washington's 2007 film *The Great Debaters.* Parks has been working with actor Mos Def, (who costarred in the Broadway production of *Topdog/Underdog,* and who also was one of the lead actors in *Fucking A,* to develop a film version of the former. One of her screenplays that was made into a film for television, and subsequently released on DVD, is her 2005 adaptation of Zora Neale Hurston's *Their Eyes Were Watching God* for Oprah Winfrey's Harpo Productions, cowritten with Mesan Sagay and Bobby Smith, Jr. and directed by Darnell Martin. Since Parks sees Hurston as an influential figure in her own work (see the discussion in the introduction), this was a significant project for her even though it was an adaptation rather than an original piece (and was co-written). She says, "It was still my work while I was following Zora Neale Hurston's path" (Parks, "An Evening").

Their Eyes tells of the coming-to-wisdom of Janie, the young African-American protagonist (played by Halle Berry), in rural Florida as she emerges from under the control of various men and discovers not only the give-and-take of real love, but how to assert a voice. From the outset (the first shot is of her bare feet walking on the road), Janie's individuality and sensuality are emphasized. When the porch-sitting gossips of Eatonville greet her with surprise upon her return, she says, "Go to hell." When they say, "What?" she responds, "I said, Afternoon, ladies." A flashback structures both the novel and the film, as Janie recounts her life story to her friend Pheoby. Janie does not intend to replicate the misadventures of Annie Tyler, another woman who ran off with her lover, only to be dumped, humiliated and penniless, by the side of the road. "Me and Tea Cake had us a real love," Janie tells Pheoby, and the rest of the story goes from her childhood and unlucky relationships with the elderly, bossy Logan Killicks (after her grandmother catches her with Johnny Taylor) and the ambitious, sexist Joe Starks, who builds and incorporates Eatonville, to her escape with Tea Cake, who dies of rabies after they are caught in a hurricane on Lake Okechobee.

Although the film makes an attempt to capture Hurston's dialogue (and Parks, with her ear for the musicality of language, is clearly the one to do so), readers of the novel will be disappointed that some of its most famous lines, such as "mah tongue is in mah friend's mouf" (referring to Janie's willingness to let Pheoby relay her story [6]), or "you got tuh *go* there tuh *know* there" [183]), are missing. Hurston uses third person and free indirect discourse to structure the frame narrative and the flashback, punctuated by Janie's first-person comments in dialogue form to Pheoby as part of the framing device. In the film, by necessity, we *see* Janie's experiences, but they are interspersed with occasional first-person voiceovers to remind us that this is all being filtered through her perspective as she recounts her tale to Pheoby. Yet the film also plays rather loosely with this idea of perspective, since we also see events in the town that Janie couldn't possibly see herself, as well as such moments as Tea Cake's POV shot of Janie when he is in the throes of rabies. The film aspires to have the spectators "go there tuh know there," identifying us with Pheoby as empathic listeners, yet its visual and other sensory details do not get us as close to Janie as the novel does.

How many of its choices were made by the director and how many by the screenwriter is difficult to determine, but the film's close attention to costumes and role-playing, hands and touching, and food—all more prominent in the film than in the novel—certainly resonates with Parks's other work. The connection between the "costume" one wears and how one is perceived (as, for example, in *Topdog/Underdog*) plays out as Janie is criticized for wearing men's overalls, as Joe Starks expects her to wear the expensive corseted dress he has ordered for her (we see the red marks it makes on her back), as Joe also forces her to wear a headwrap (in the film, her hair dangles temptingly over the checkerboard at the general store), and so forth. At the end, Janie clutches Tea Cake's denim workshirt, a tangible reminder of what he meant to her. Hands form a central image in Parks's *Last Black Man*, in which the Black Man's moving of his hands is his gesture for moving to the next world and in which And Bigger and Bigger asks to have his hands freed. In the film of *Their Eyes*, hands also mark moments of sensuality and transition: Janie's and Joe's hands touch while they are still in love, Janie closes Joe's eyes when he has died, and Janie's and Tea Cake's hands are together on the piano when he is teaching her how to play. *Last Black Man*, as we have seen, also contains multiple and resonant images of food. Food in the film of *Their Eyes* becomes emblematic of problematized versions of nurturing. Janie (who is starving) digs voraciously into the pie that Pheoby has brought her as a gesture of their friendship. When Joe has consigned her to the role of the Mayor's Wife, we see match cuts of the trays of food that she has to prepare and bring him over a period of twenty years. This is set up in contrast to the freedom associated with Tea Cake, whose name itself implies a treat. He rubs lemon on her lips, they eat fish right out of the skillet, Janie places shrimp between Tea Cake's lips as they dance together and eat other delicacies when they have become part of the creolized community of migrant workers at Lake Okechobee.

The title of Hurston's novel comes from a moment when both animals and humans are fleeing the hurricane. The hurricane is a force of nature that overrides all, and Hurston describes those who have decided to wait it out, as the wind gathers, "their souls asking if He meant to measure their puny might against His. They seemed to be staring at the dark, but their eyes were watching God" (151). When the hurricane arrives, it is characterized in apocalyptic terms as a great equalizer: "Wind and rain beating on old folks and beating on babies . . . Common danger made common friends. Nothing sought a conquest over the other" (155–56). Strikingly, the film does not play this out, nor does it include Janie's earlier thoughts about Death: "What need has Death for a cover, and what winds can blow against him? He stands in his high house that overlooks the world" (80). For Hurston, the images of God and Death represent an all-consuming power. Henry Louis Gates Jr., in his analysis of discourse in the novel, argues for its "transcendent" effect, calling the narrative "a lyrical and disembodied yet individual voice, from which emerges a singular longing and utterance, a transcendent, ultimately racial self, extending far beyond the merely individual" (183). The film revises all of this into what one might describe as the more Oprah-like images of the self-determined woman. When Janie looks upward at the gathering hurricane clouds and Tea Cake asks her what she is doing, she replies, "I'm watching God" (an individual rather than a collective act), and we hear these lines again in voiceover as she floats in her favorite pond and looks skyward in the closing shot of the film. The vision of "God" that Hurston depicts as omnipotent and threatening becomes associated, in the film, with Janie's embracing sensuality as part of her movement into self-discovery. It follows implicitly from her earlier comment (in the novel, but not the film) that women have their own way of talking to God. This closing scene reflects Parks's interest in resurrection, as Janie has had to die, in a manner of speaking, and be reborn at the end (as she is also rebaptized upon entering the water again). The end of the novel emphasizes the continual resurrection of Tea Cake in Janie's memory as well: "He could never be dead until she herself had finished feeling and thinking" (183). As we recall, Billy's sense of affirmation at the end of *Getting Mother's Body* comes from recognizing simply that we're all going to die, but "there's stops in between there and now." The ending of the film of *Their Eyes* is far less ambiguous than that of *Girl 6*; the protagonist has successfully remained true to her own vision of herself. But it also subsumes Hurston's image of Janie as active gatherer of experience—"She pulled in her horizon like a great fish-net" (184)—to the impression that she has moved into a kind of self-absorbed spirituality.

Musical Projects

Parks's plays have always been informed by a musical sensibility, from the jazz-influenced "rep and rev" style to the blues songs in *Topdog/Underdog*. *Fucking A* is structured with Brechtian-style songs that provide humorous and sometimes-surprising encounters between Hester and other characters, and the audience. As noted previously, her novel *Getting Mother's Body* is deeply informed by the blues, and Parks has recorded a CD of the songs from the novel.

What readers or theatergoers may not know, though, is that she also has been involved with musical theater projects. In 2002, she worked with author William Gibson on a concert musical adaptation of Clifford Odets's play *Golden Boy.* "That rarely happens," Margo Jefferson comments, "that an African American woman takes material that has been authored originally by whites and gets her chance to put her mark on it" (qtd. in Rasbury 1). For several years, Parks worked on *Hoopz,* a musical for Disney Theatrical Productions about the Harlem Globetrotters. The project was originally to be created by slam poet Reg E. Gaines and choreographer Savion Glover, but Parks and Jeanine Tesori (who teamed up with Tony Kushner on *Caroline, or Change*) took it over ("Broadway: Lost in Development"). As Terry Berliner explains in an essay about musicals that have not been produced, "Disney musicals are mythological in proportion and rely on a great deal of fantasy"—which also means that they are expensive. At this point, *Hoopz* has not made it out of development (54–55). Another project is a stage musical about Ray Charles, from the producers who created the very successful film biography *Ray* (Parks, "An Evening"). One future direction of her work, then, will include experiments, adaptations, and collaborations in musical genres.

365 Days/365 Plays and into the Future

> ARJUNA. Where to?
> KRISHNA. Does it matter?
> ARJUNA. Yeah. Because I have a choice in the matter, and if we're going somewhere I dont like, I may choose not to go.
>
>   —Parks, *Start Here* (*365 Days/365 Plays* 3)

Revivals of Parks's plays continue to be mounted internationally, particularly *Venus* (which has been staged in South Africa, among many other places) and *Topdog/Underdog* (which has seen important productions at Chicago's Steppenwolf Theatre and other venues). Some of her earlier works deserve restagings that might lead to better understandings of their innovative dramatic riches: *The America Play* in particular comes to mind. Parks, unlike some other playwrights (notoriously, Samuel Beckett), believes in giving directors freedom to work with her texts, and this promises exciting and surprising interpretations of her earlier drama.

As this is written, Parks's major project for the 2006–7 theatrical season nears completion. Beginning on November 13, 2002, she took on the self-imposed challenge of writing a play a day for a year, some long and some short; she says, "I just wrote them. It was enough for me to just show up every day. What was going on that day didn't matter" (Gener 10).

> I was writing a play every day, whatever happened. Whether I was busy or not, whether it was good or not, whether it was convenient or not. Whatever happened. And it became this prayer, almost. To theatre. To life. To the art process, the process of making art and being alive. (Als 76)

Bonnie Metzgar, who worked with Parks to set a production scheme into motion, remarks:

> As I read through the complete cycle, I was struck by this amazing space that Suzan-Lori made for herself, to connect to art at the center of her life every day. . . . It was this very intimate thing between her and her muse, but I started imagining what it might be to try to turn that intimacy outward. (Walat 27)

The resulting project, *365 Days/365 Plays*, was produced as the collaborative effort of over seven hundred theaters across the United States, including New York's Public Theater, Atlanta's Alliance Theatre Company, the Seattle Repertory Theatre, and Los Angeles's Center Theater Group/Mark Taper Forum. In New York alone, fifty-two theaters planned to put on one week's worth of the plays (Robertson, "Public" B2). Fourteen "hub" and many "satellite" theaters covered the country, and there was an additional network of university theaters. In order to democratize the availability of the pieces, Parks and Metzgar set the licensing fees in most cases at a dollar a play (Green 264), and also stipulated that no admission be charged. Individual troupes were encouraged to seek nontheatrical venues; when the New Georges Theater performed the March 19–25 plays, for instance, they said, "Interested in the portability of the plays, we brought them to people, rather than having people come to us. We performed in private spaces, primarily offices during the workday— conference rooms, office foyers, an elevator lobby, a youth hostel, and a private home" (*365 NYC* Program 5).

Needless to say, no previous playwright has attempted such an ambitious project (Parks says, "Like Lance Armstrong, I'm good at climbing hills" [Gener 11]), but the willingness of theaters across the country to participate speaks volumes about the recognition of her skill and importance as a dramatist. The *New York Times* said that the project "may be the largest and most elaborate theatrical premiere ever," explaining that it involved not only "prominent institutional theaters" but also "summer-stock theaters in Montana, community ensembles on the South Side of Chicago, a nursing home in Atlanta and an abandoned movie house in the valley of the Rio Grande" (Robertson, "What Do You Get," B3).

Despite the huge number of short plays in the cycle, there is a distinct continuity in styles and themes both from Parks's previous works and within the cycle itself. The work is surprisingly coherent despite its unconventional approach and its reliance on immediate events for inspiration (anything from the LA celebrity culture of *Meeting Brad Pitt* to a holiday, or the writer's birthday, or going through airport security). Like Carol Lay's *Story Minute* comic strips, the pieces are self-contained microdramas, yet they complement one another. At times, Parks's own previous plays form the inspiration for a piece; in *Too Close* (September 4), the characters speak in TALK as they did in *Fucking A,* and another (August 11) is about the closing of *Topdog/Underdog* on Broadway and its opening in London (283). The cycle remains true to Parks's style, with "spells," "rests," her unorthodox spelling techniques, and so forth. Her interest in music resurfaces continually: some of the characters sing blues or other types of songs, and Glenn Gould as interpreter of Bach is a character. Death is a recurrent motif; at times the plays commemorate famous people who have just passed on to the next world (Gregory Hines, Carol Shields, John Ritter, George Plimpton, etc.). A critical and sometimes satirical or sardonic view of black culture and history, while less in evidence than in some of her earlier works, still informs the pieces—she asks, for example, why February, Black History Month, happens to be the shortest month and presents characters like Afrodite Jackson Jones (300). Many of the pieces are about couples or family relationships, including references to Parks's brother's birthday, and there are multiple parent-child minidramas, particularly (as shall be discussed shortly) a *Father Comes Home from the Wars* series.

Indeed, this type of repetition is one of the most enjoyable aspects of the cycle: for readers (or potentially, viewers) of the entire work, it comes partly in the form of the various characters and "epic installments" that resurface, such as *Father Comes Home*, continued appearances by Abraham Lincoln and Mary Todd Lincoln, and others. There are also three "Constants" that Parks says can be performed at any and all points in the cycle: *Remember Who You Are*, *Action in Inaction*, and *Inaction in Action*. But any readers or audience members who see a given week or month of the cycle will also be rewarded by the amusing carryovers from one play to another. They may be as simple as the set from one turning into the set for another. At times, though, just when we think that Parks has disposed of characters in one drama, they return in another. These two strategies are combined when, for instance, a red carpet that is rolled out on November 28 ends up as part of the set on November 30 and December 1; then on December 7, the women soldiers Bertie and Dolly who tended it back on November 28 emerge again.

The setting of the pieces in *365 Plays* is often a bare stage or a kind of nowhere-space; this is partially for practical reasons, as Parks wants the directors and designers of the performances to use their own creativity in putting them together. More than that, though, what we frequently see in the pieces is a kind of dystopian, possibly sci-fi or futuristic (or alternate) world, as we did in *Fucking A:* the plays return repeatedly to environments in which the characters' distorted behavior is a parodically warped version of the way we might imagine real political life shaping us. In *The News Is Here*, for example, a man and woman fight over whether to leave a baby out on the street that may be a "Mountainite": "So, even if we could sell him, we'd be responsible for the carnage he'd cause" (78). In conjunction with these stripped-down, dystopian settings, often the visuals depend on lines, rows, processions, and other group formations: even more so than in some of her earlier works, Parks is aware of the instant power of the image, perhaps all the more so because each short play needs to make its point very quickly. In many of the pieces—such as *Even in a House Like This* (pairs of Kissers and Watchers), *Live Free or Die* (a version of Red Rover), or *All Things Being Equal* (which features competing monarchs)—patterns or visual repetitions and formations register for the audience much in the way that a painting or sculpture would.

As might be expected if one takes on the challenge of writing a play every single day for a year, the difficulty of the project itself sometimes takes center stage: we see the Writer arguing with her Editor, or the title itself announces that *This Is Probably Not a Play* (December 16) or even *This Is Shit* (December 23). In the latter, when a Program Thrower stands up and announces the words of the title and exits in disgust, the rest of the audience gives a standing ovation. Blurring the boundaries between audience and characters, and incorporating the act of wrestling with the creative process in many of the pieces, allows Parks the freedom to keep experimenting—and more than that, when a week or a month of the cycle is presented in repertory, it allows for a Pirandellian reminder to the spectators that what they are witnessing challenges the notion that "real life" and "performance" can be separated.

Occasionally, the classics make an appearance, though always with a twist: we see Shakespeare's *Hamlet* conflated with William Faulkner's *The Hamlet* (87), or Oedipus, Tantalus, Cassandra, and Clytemnestra as guests on the *Jerry Springer Show* (167). Parks also plays recurrently upon fairy tales and folktales, at least in part as a way of forcing the happy-ending formula to collide with the (literal or sometimes metaphorical) violence with which her short pieces must come to a close. To give just one example, the final stage directions for *Dragon Keeper* (March 11) indicate:

> Then the Dragon screams with joy. Fires and Armageddon. Eons pass within an instant. God blinks the Great Eye and, as the world is born anew and creation rapidly surges forward, evolution happens double-triple time. We're all caught up to where we were just before the play started, but this time, instead of burning, we'll continue to sleep, unaware of our power. (150)

Even more prevalently, one can see a clear influence of Samuel Beckett's own short dramas, with the minimalist and often abstract or metaphorical imagery (August 27 and 28, for example, feature slave and master characters, each tied to the end of a rope). The influence of Gertrude Stein is again evident as well, both in the language games and in the constant interest in subverting the "rules" of the theatrical genre. In this respect, many of the pieces in the cycle also resemble the works of the European surrealists like Tristan Tzara and Antonin Artaud, both of whom wrote dramas in which the "stage-able" is constantly challenged by replacing characters with body parts, having the stage go up in flames, and so forth; it is not uncommon for Parks to instruct us, for instance, that a character's action goes on "forever," or to replace characters per se with "figures" (as she did in *Last Black Man*). For example, the speaker in *The Great Wave off Kanagawa* is the wave itself (230). One of her favorite techniques is to take a cliché or other verbal formula and to render it as literally as possible, as in *You Wouldnt Want to Take It with You Even If You Could* (127) or in *The Presidents Day Sale*, where former presidents are actually being sold (128).

There is a striking tension between the brevity of the plays and the indication Parks often makes at the end of a piece that it repeats itself or goes on in perpetuity: the closing stage directions of *Everybody's Got an Aunt Jemimah* (May 10), for instance, explain that the characters' discussion should "go on forever" (204). Many of the pieces end abruptly, as might be expected from the nature of the blackout-play genre (cf. the works by the Neo-Futurist troupe, whose New York branch staged a week of *365 Plays*, in their *Too Much Light Makes the Baby Go Blind*). In some ways, though, the throwing of the ending into a *mise-en-abîme* also conjures up Parks's beloved "hole" imagery as well as challenging the idea that what we see on stage in a given moment has the expected boundaries of performance time only.

As mentioned earlier, one of the plays that continues in installments throughout the cycle is *Father Comes Home from the Wars*. In each of these, as the Father figure arrives home, he encounters a different type of psychological block, reassimilation problem, or relationship obstacle (all of which tend to be presented in abstract or metaphorical fashion). Part 1, for instance, features Mother—who did not expect his return—asking him to go out and come back in again, and in Part 3, he has to deal with Junior saying, "Im gonna be a soldier just like yr a soldier, right, Pop?" (147). The link here is to the last section of Parks's *Imperceptible Mutabilities*; as with Sergeant Smith in that play, the returning soldier's estrangement from himself and his family is at least partially rooted in Parks's own experiences growing up in a military family. At the same time, the short *Father Comes Home* pieces take on an additional resonance—as do quite a few other pieces in the cycle—when considered in the context of the ongoing war in Iraq. The plays for March in particular are filled with imagery that asks us to question blind prowar sentiments and the stepping up (at the time Parks was writing the pieces) of violence in the Middle East: in *No War*, One Person tells the crowd that chanting "No war!" isn't a play, but they continue chanting anyway, and in *The Act of Forgiveness*, an Antiwar Protestor is pointed out to a group of kids who remark upon him as "Ancient History" and "Old school" (156–57).

A favorite Parks character who reappears throughout the cycle is, of course, Abraham Lincoln, who figures prominently in *The America Play* and *Topdog/Underdog* (see discussion in the chapter on those plays). While Lincoln himself turns up as subject several times (as in *The Birth of Abraham Lincoln* on Lincoln's birthday, or *The*

Mr. Lincoln Rose [April 12]), here, Mary Todd Lincoln (a subject of fascination in part because the real person was said to have been crazy) also gets her say. In *Mrs. Keckley and Mrs. Lincoln*, Mary argues with her black dressmaker, Mrs. Keckley (a real figure) about what to wear for the evening; the piece ends with yet another echo of the assassination as Mary comments that they are going to see the play *Our American Cousin* that night and that it's "A comedy! We are the lucky ones, Mrs. Keckley!" (27). Similarly, in *Abraham Lincoln at 89* (December 2), when the president explains that he is celebrating his eighty-ninth birthday because he may not live to one hundred, Mary points out, "He didnt live to be 89 either, truth be told" (40). Mary seems to be somewhat of a visionary, rather than the unstable first lady that historical narrative has generally made her.

Finally, one recurrent motif that is entirely apropos to Parks's work is digging and holes (her annotation for *Holey* on March 8 says, "Another one of my hole plays. Don't ask why" [386]). The imagery suggests the struggle to create the plays themselves: the need to keep "digging" for more material, and the playwright's fear of having gotten herself into a "hole" by having taken on the project. The aforementioned *Holey* is about a Woman who explains that her ego has fallen into the hole and she is waiting for it to be retrieved. As discussed earlier in this study, though, the interest in digging and holes also evokes sexuality, death, resurrection, and history—all thrown into a kind of bottomless pit, shades of Beckett, that forces a new kind of archaeological practice, a new way of "digging" the past to look at the world. A potential romance develops between a Man who's an "agitator" and a woman (not yet dead) whom he digs up in *Hole* (Nov. 27). And on July 10, two writers described as being a lot like Suzan-Lori Parks and William Faulkner (Simone and Walter) are quite literally "digging Bach," taking turns with the shovel (250): they connect through the past, but they also create something different through their mutual inspiration.

Parks wrote "New Black Math," which was published in the December 2005 issue of *Theatre Journal*, as a sequel to her earlier essay "An Equation for Black People Onstage," and it appears as part of a Forum on Black Theatre in the journal, but it also contains a miniplay (or perhaps two). She explains that she composed the piece in August 2005 in the sobering aftermath of both Hurricane Katrina and the imminent death (from cancer) of playwright August Wilson. The piece is a series of declarations, often contradictory, about what constitutes "a black play," full of puns and political statements: "A black play is late. / A black play is RIGHT ON and RIGHT ON TIME" (576). One of its more controversial elements is the insistence that a black play may not be what one thinks; she says that *The Glass Menagerie* and *Angels in America* are both "black plays." She entitles the miniplay in the middle of the piece *The Bridge*, and it begins as a dialogue between Momma and her husband, Yo, clearly in the post-Katrina context of waiting to be rescued from their house, which is under water. After the essay has already resumed, she interrupts it again with an intermission which is really another miniplay, in which Sister on the Street and Brother on the Corner argue about what it means for the essay to have turned into a diatribe, interrupted by the Black Playwright as a character herself, who asks for some change to call up Harriet Tubman, Nat Turner, John Brown, Frederick Douglass, and Sojourner Truth. The Black Playwright figure adds:

> Audiences still ask "what do black people think about such and such?" Black people think the world is fucked. Thats what black people think. Black people dont always use apostrophes neither. Black people took the rallying cry "burn baby burn" and turned it into the chorus of "Disco Interno" and some of us danced all the way to the bank, thats what black people think. Black people know there is a war going on against our blackness and somehow we've been enlisted to fight on the front lines. (581)

The piece is obviously a provocative one, and some will argue that Parks is being disingenuous in her series of avowals and contradictions. What she is undertaking, though, is a sophisticated set of responses to the accusation she has faced over the years that her plays are not "black enough," that in characters like Booth and Lincoln she is not creating "role models," and so on. Her response reflects what John Ernest, also using the math metaphor, calls the "need to enter into an understanding of racial constructions that is chaotic rather than Euclidean" (49). In this essay-play, Parks uses Signifying to play with the slippages and elusiveness of Defining Black Theatre. The series of contradictions that some will say doesn't add up to anything does precisely that: it shows, performatively, how the meaning of a "black play" is caught up in these oppositions, these in-your-face statements, these resistances to being pinned down.

In 1990, when Parks was first achieving recognition as a playwright for works that were seen as highly experimental and avant-garde, Alisa Solomon commented in a major discussion of Parks:

> As she is increasingly recognized, she too—as she well knows—will run the risk of seeing white institutions want to fix that flattening –d onto her roun writing . . . Parks has the social consciousness and, perhaps more important, the talent to stick to her experimental/political guns. But I fear she'll find herself stuck in the crossfire of a theater ever torn between the call of exciting new work and the sleepy demands of a subscription base. It's hard to predict whether Parks's work will find its rightful place in the absence of a social movement addressing the issues she so artfully explores. . . . The uptown audience might *never* ask Parks about form. But if they are lucky enough to see her plays, they'll experience her thrilling refiguring of the concept of theater. (80)

Years later, Parks has indeed gone on to find mainstream success (a play on Broadway, the Pulitzer Prize, screenplays for Oprah, etc.). While Queen-then-Pharaoh Hatshepsut in *Last Black Man* worries about having had her "mark" erased, Parks herself has made a permanent mark on the theater. Much to her credit, however, she has never hesitated to take risks: by venturing into new genres, by trying broad-based experiments such as the *365 Plays* project, and mostly by continuing to speak in a theatrical voice that is truly her own. We are all the luckier for it.

List of Premieres

The Sinner's Place (unofficial staging of senior honors thesis play), Mt. Holyoke College, 1984

Betting on the Dust Commander, dir. Suzan-Lori Parks, The Gas Station, New York City, 1987; dir. Liz Diamond, Company One, Hartford, Connecticut, 1990 and Working Theater, New York City, 1991

Imperceptible Mutabilities in the Third Kingdom, dir. Liz Diamond, workshop production at BACA Downtown, Brooklyn, 1988; world premiere at BACA Fringe Festival, September 1989; one section, *Greeks*, dir. Diamond, at Manhattan Theater Club's Downtown/Uptown Festival, 1991

The Death of the Last Black Man in the Whole Entire World, dir. Beth A. Schachter, staged reading at New York Theatre Workshop's "Mondays at Three" series, Perry Street Theater, 1989–1990 season; premiere dir. Schachter, BACA Downtown, Brooklyn, September 1990; new prod. dir. Liz Diamond, Yale Repertory Theater, 1992

Pickling (radio play), New American Radio, 1990; stage version dir. Allison Eve Zell, Harlem Summer Arts Festival, New York City, 1998; restaged (all dir. Zell) at the Lincoln Center Directors Lab at HERE Arts Center, 1999; at The Mint Space, 2000; at Joe's Pub, Joseph Papp Public Theater, 2001; and at the Cherry Lane Theater, New York City, 2002

Devotees in the Garden of Love, dir. Oskar Eustis, Actors Theatre of Louisville Humana Festival, 1992

The America Play, dir. Liz Diamond, commissioned by Theater for a New Audience; given workshop productions at Arena Stage and Dallas Theatre Center in 1993; premiered in New York City at the Joseph Papp Public Theater as a coproduction of the New York Shakespeare Festival, Yale Repertory Theater, and Theater for a New Audience, February 1994

Venus, dir. Richard Foreman, commissioned by the Women's Project, premiered at the Joseph Papp Public Theater, New York City, April 1996

In the Blood, dir. David Esbjornson, Joseph Papp Public Theater, New York City, November 1999

Fucking A, dir. Suzan-Lori Parks and the Infernal Bridegroom Company, DiverseWorks/Infernal Bridegroom Productions, DiverseWorks Artspace, Houston, February 2000; dir. Michael Greif, Joseph Papp Public Theater, New York City, March 2003

Topdog/Underdog, dir. George C. Wolfe, Joseph Papp Public Theater, New York City, July 2001; transferred to Ambassador Theater, New York City (Broadway), April 2002

365 Days/365 Plays. Yearlong play cycle opened at the Joseph Papp Public Theater, New York City, and other venues across the United States, beginning November 13, 2006.

Works Cited

Primary Sources

Parks, Suzan-Lori. *The America Play and Other Works [Imperceptible Mutabilities in the Third Kingdom, Betting on the Dust Commander, Pickling, The Death of the Last Black Man in the Whole Entire World, Devotees in the Garden of Love, The America Play]*. New York: TCG, 1995.

Parks, Suzan-Lori. "From *Elements of Style*." *The America Play and Other Works*. New York: TCG, 1995. 6–18.

Parks, Suzan-Lori. "An Equation for Black People Onstage." *The America Play and Other Works*. New York: TCG, 1995. 19–22.

Parks, Suzan-Lori. "An Evening with Suzan-Lori Parks." Presentation and discussion at DePauw University, 19 April 2006.

Parks, Suzan-Lori. *Getting Mother's Body*. New York: Random, 2003.

Parks, Suzan-Lori. *Girl 6* (screenplay). Dir. Spike Lee. Perf. Theresa Randle, Isaiah Washington, Spike Lee. Fox Searchlight/40 Acres & a Mule Productions. 1996.

Parks, Suzan-Lori. "New Black Math." *Theatre Journal* 57.4 (December 2005): 576–83.

Parks, Suzan-Lori. "Possession." *The America Play and Other Works*. New York: TCG, 1995. 3–5.

Parks, Suzan-Lori. *The Red Letter Plays [In the Blood and Fucking A]*. New York: TCG, 2001.

Parks, Suzan-Lori. *The Songs from Getting Mother's Body*. CD. Perf. Suzan-Lori Parks and Paul Oscher. Mama's Helper Music, BMI, 2004.

Parks, Suzan-Lori. *Their Eyes Were Watching God* (screenplay, co-scr. Misan Sagay and Bobby Smith, Jr.) Dir. Darnell Martin. Perf. Halle Berry, Ruben Santiago-Hudson, Michael Ealy. Harpo Productions. 2005.

Parks, Suzan-Lori. *365 Days/365 Plays*. New York: TCG, 2006.

Parks, Suzan-Lori. *Topdog/Underdog*. New York: TCG, 2001.

Parks, Suzan-Lori. *Venus*. New York: TCG, 1997.

Secondary Sources

Acker, Kathy. *Blood and Guts in High School*. New York: Grove, 1989.

Alcott, Louisa May. *Eight Cousins*. Boston: Little, Brown, 1996.

Alcott, Louisa May. *Little Women*. New York: Airmont, 1966.

Alexander, Elizabeth. *The Venus Hottentot*. St. Paul, MN: Graywolf, 1990.

Als, Hilton. "The Show-Woman." *New Yorker*, October 30, 2006, 74–81.

Altman, Susan. *The Encyclopedia of African-American Heritage*. New York: Facts on File, 1997.

"Another Hester, a Different 'A.'" *USA Today*, March 26, 2003, 4D.

Backalenick, Irene. "Suzan-Lori Parks: The Joy of Playwrighting." *Theater Week*, April 8–14, 1996, 27–28.

Baker-White, Robert. "Questioning the Ground of American Identity: George Pierce Baker's *The Pilgrim Spirit* and Suzan-Lori Parks's *The America Play*." *Journal of American Drama and Theatre* 12 (Spring 2000): 71–89.

Baldwin, James. *Notes of a Native Son*. 1955. Boston: Beacon Press, 1984.

Beckett, Samuel. *Collected Shorter Plays*. New York: Grove, 1984.

Beckett, Samuel. *Waiting for Godot*. New York: Grove, 1954.

Ben-Zvi, Linda. "'Aroun the Worl': The Signifyin(g) Theater of Suzan-Lori Parks." *The Theatrical Gamut: Notes for a Post-Beckettian Stage*. Ed. Enoch Brater. Ann Arbor: University of Michigan Press, 1995. 189–208.

Bercovitch, Sacvan. *The Office of the Scarlet Letter*. Baltimore: Johns Hopkins University Press, 1991.

Berlant, Lauren. *The Anatomy of National Fantasy: Hawthorne, Utopia, and Everyday Life*. Chicago: University of Chicago Press, 1991.

Berliner, Terry. "The Hitmakers: Commercial Producing." *American Theater* 23.4 (April 2006): 30–31, 51–55.

Bernal, Martin. *Black Athena: The Afroasiatic Roots of Classical Civilization*. New Brunswick, NJ: Rutgers University Press, 1987.

Bernard, Louise. "The Musicality of Language: Redefining History in Suzan-Lori Parks's *The Death of the Last Black Man in the Whole Entire World*." *African American Review* 31.4 (Winter 1997): 687–98.

Brantley, Ben. "Not to Worry, Mr. Lincoln, It's Just a Con Game." *New York Times*, April 8, 2002, www.nytimes.com/200 . . . 8TOPD.html (visited January 16, 2006).

Brecht, Bertolt. *Mother Courage*. Trans. Eric Bentley. New York: Grove, 1966.

Brewer, Mary F. *Staging Whiteness*. Middletown, CT: Wesleyan University Press, 2005.

"Broadway: Lost in Development." www.jimsdeli.com/theater/lost/default.htm (visited January 1, 2008).

"Brothers, Hounded by History." Review of *Topdog/Underdog*. *USA Today*, April 8, 2002, 3D.

Bruce, Mary Grant. *A Little Bush Maid*. 1910. digital.libupenn.edu/women/bruce/maid/maid-XVIII.html (visited January 16, 2006).

Brustein, Robert. "The Element of Surprise." *New Republic*, January 24, 2000, 31–33.

Brustein, Robert. "A Homeboy Godot." *New Republic*, May 13, 2002, 25–26.

Bryant, Aaron. "Broadway, Her Way." *(New) Crisis* 109.2 (March–April 2002): 43–45.

Bullock, Kurt. "Famous/Last Words: The Disruptive Rhetoric of Historico-Narrative 'Finality' in Suzan-Lori Parks' *The America Play.*" *American Drama* 10.2 (June 2001): 69–87.

Chase-Riboud, Barbara. *Hottentot Venus.* New York: Anchor, 2003.

Chaudhuri, Una. "For Posterior's Sake." Interview with Suzan-Lori Parks. *Public Access* (stagebill), May 1996, 34–36.

Chaudhuri, Una. *Staging Place: The Geography of Modern Drama.* Ann Arbor: University of Michigan Press, 1995.

Chaudhuri, Una. Review of *Topdog/Underdog.* Public Theater, New York City, July 14, 2001. *Theatre Journal* 54.2 (May 2002): 289–91.

Christian, Barbara. "Fixing Methodologies: *Beloved.*" *Female Subjects in Black and White.* Ed. Elizabeth Abel, Barbara Christian, and Helene Moglen. Berkeley and Los Angeles: University of California Press, 1997. 363–70.

Curry, Vicki. Interview with Suzan-Lori Parks. "Life and Times" (KCET TV), June 20, 2003. http://www.kcet.org/lifeandtimes/archives/200306/20030620.php (visited January 1, 2008).

Dickens, Charles. *Little Dorrit.* New York: Dutton, 1969.

Dixon, Kimberly D. "'An I am Sheba me am (She be doo be wah waaah doo wah') O(au)rality, Textuality and Performativity: African American Literature's Vernacular Theory and the Work of Suzan-Lori Parks." *Journal of American Drama and Theatre* 11.1 (Winter 1998): 49–66.

Douglass, Frederick E. *Narrative of the Life of Frederick Douglass.* New York: Signet, 1997.

Drukman, Steven. "Suzan-Lori Parks and Liz Diamond: Doo-a-diddly-dit-dit." *TDR* 39.3 (Fall 1995): 56–75.

Elam, Harry J., Jr., and Alice Rayner. "Body Parts: Between Story and Spectacle in *Venus* by Suzan-Lori Parks." *Staging Resistance: Essays on Political Theater.* Ed. Jeanne Colleran and Jenny S. Spencer. Ann Arbor: University of Michigan Press, 1998. 265–82.

Elam, Harry J., Jr., and Alice Rayner. "Echoes from the Black (W)hole: An Examination of *The America Play* by Suzan-Lori Parks." *Performing America: Cultural Nationalism in American Theater.* Ed. Jeffrey D. Mason and J. Ellen Gainor. Ann Arbor: University of Michigan Press, 1999. 178–92.

Ernest, John. "Race Walks in the Room: White Teachers in Black Studies." *White Scholars/African American Texts.* Ed. Lisa A. Long. New Brunswick, NJ: Rutgers University Press, 2005. 40–51.

Faulkner, William. *As I Lay Dying.* New York: Vintage, 1990.

Feingold, Michael. "Carnival Knowledge." *Village Voice,* May 14, 1996, 81.

Fornes, Maria Irene. *Plays.* New York: PAJ, 1986.

Foucault, Michel. *Discipline and Punish: The Birth of the Prison.* Trans. Alan Sheridan. New York: Vintage, 1995.

Fraden, Rena. "A Mid-Life Cultural Crisis: Chiastic Criticism and Encounters with the Theatrical Work of Suzan-Lori Parks." *Journal of American Drama and Theatre* 17.3 (Fall 2005): 36–56.

Frank, Haike. "The Instability of Meaning in Suzan-Lori Parks's *The America Play.*" *American Drama* 11.2 (Summer 2002): 4–20.

Foster, Verna. "Suzan-Lori Parks's Staging of the Lincoln Myth in *The America Play* and *Topdog/Underdog.*" *Journal of American Drama and Theatre* 17.3 (Fall 2005): 24–35.

Frieze, James. "*Imperceptible Mutabilities in the Third Kingdom:* Suzan-Lori Parks and the Shared Struggle to Perceive." *Modern Drama* 41 (Winter 1998): 523–32.

Garrett, Shawn-Marie. "The Possession of Suzan-Lori Parks." *American Theater* 17.8 (October 2000): 22–26, 132–34.

Gates, Anita. "Lincoln's Sadness Equaled His Greatness." *New York Times,* January 16, 2006, B11.

Gates, Henry Louis, Jr. *The Signifying Monkey: A Theory of African-American Literary Criticism.* New York: Oxford University Press, 1988.

Geis, Deborah R. *Postmodern Theatric(k)s: Monologue in Contemporary American Drama.* Ann Arbor: University of Michigan Press, 1993.

Gener, Randy. "One Nation, under Suzan-Lori Parks." *American Theater* 23.4 (April 2006): 10–11.

Glueck, Grace. "The Woman Who Ruled Egypt as King, Not Queen." *New York Times,* March 31, 2006, B27, B30.

Gollin, Rita K. "'Again a Literary Man': Vocation and *The Scarlet Letter.*" *Critical Essays on Hawthorne's The Scarlet Letter.* Ed. David B. Kesterson. Boston: G. K. Hall, 1988. 171–83.

Green, Jesse. "A Play a Day." *Elle,* October 2006, 264.

Greenblatt, Stephen J. *Learning to Curse: Essays in Early Modern Culture.* New York: Routledge, 1990.

Hawthorne, Nathaniel. *The Scarlet Letter.* New York: Holt, Rinehart and Winston, 1963.

Henderson, John. "The Birth of Chocolate or, The Tree of the Food of the Gods." *Arts & Sciences* (Cornell University newsletter), Fall 2001, 1–2.

hooks, bell. *Bone Black.* New York: Henry Holt, 1996.

hooks, bell. "Eating the Other: Desire and Resistance." *Eating Culture.* Ed. Ron Scapp and Brian Seitz. Albany: SUNY Press, 1998. 181–200.

hooks, bell. *We Real Cool: Black Men and Masculinity.* New York: Routledge, 2004.

Hurston, Zora Neale. *Their Eyes Were Watching God.* 1937. New York: Harper Perennial, 1990.

Ionesco, Eugène. *The Bald Soprano. Four Plays by Eugene Ionesco.* Trans. Donald M. Allen. New York: Grove, 1958. 7–42.

Jacobus, Lee. "Interview with Suzan-Lori Parks" and "Interview with Liz Diamond." *The Bedford Introduction to Drama.* Fourth ed. Boston: Bedford/St. Martin's, 2001. 1632–36.

Jefferson, Margo. "The Feel of Real Life Working Its Magic." *New York Times*, April 21, 2002, 9, 22.

Jiggetts, Shelby. "Interview with Suzan-Lori Parks." *Callaloo* 19.2 (Spring 1996): 309–17.

Johung, Jennifer. "Figuring the 'Spells'/Spelling the Figures: Suzan-Lori Parks's 'Scene of Love (?).'" *Theatre Journal* 58.1 (March 2006): 39–52.

Joyce, James. *Ulysses.* New York: Vintage, 1961.

Kaufman, Moises. *Gross Indecency: The Three Trials of Oscar Wilde.* New York: Vintage, 1997.

Keats, John. "Ode on a Grecian Urn." *The Mentor Book of Major British Poets.* Ed. Oscar Williams. New York: Penguin Putnam, 1963. 196–97.

Kennedy, Adrienne. *Adrienne Kennedy in One Act.* Minneapolis. University of Minnesota Press, 1988.

Kennedy, Adrienne. *People Who Led to My Plays.* New York: TCG, 1987.

Lahr, John. "Lowdown Sensations." *New Yorker*, May 20, 1996, 98.

Lamont, Rosette C. "Introduction." *Women on the Verge: Seven Avant Garde Plays.* New York: Applause, 1993. vii–xxxvi.

Lay, Carol. *Strip Joint.* Northampton, MA: Kitchen Sink, 1998.

Lewis, Leslie W. "Naming the Problem Embedded in the Problem That Led to the Question 'Who Shall Teach African American Literature?'" *White Scholars/African American Texts.* Ed. Lisa A. Long. New Brunswick, NJ: Rutgers University Press, 2005. 52–67.

Louis, Yvette. "Body Language: The Black Female Body and the Word in Suzan-Lori Parks's *The Death of the Last Black Man in the Whole Entire World.*" *Recovering the Black Female Body: Self-Representations by African American Women.* Ed. Michael Bennett and Vanessa D. Dickerson. New Brunswick, NJ: Rutgers University Press, 2001. 141–64.

"The Making of *Girl 6.*" *Girl 6.* Feature on *Girl 6* (DVD). Dir. Spike Lee. Perf. Theresa Randle, Isaiah Washington, Spike Lee. 1996. Starz/Anchor Bay 2006.

Malkin, Jeanette R. *Memory-Theater and Postmodern Drama.* Ann Arbor: University of Michigan Press, 1999.

Maslin, Janet. "Finding a Career in Telephone Sex." *New York Times*, March 22, 1996, C3.

Mason, Keith Antar. *for black boys who have considered homicide when the streets were too much. Colored Contradictions.* Ed. Harry J. Elam and Robert Alexander. New York: Plume, 1996. 175–253.

McGreal, Chris. "Coming Home." *The Guardian,* February 21, 2002. http://www.education.guardian.co.uk/Print/0,3858,4360082,00.html (visited May 27, 2003).

Miller, Greg. "The Bottom of Desire in Suzan-Lori Parks's *Venus.*" *Modern Drama* 45, no. 1 (spring 2002): 125–37.

Miller, Samantha, and Sharon Cotliar. "Best in Show." *People,* June 3, 2002, 143–44.

Moglen, Helene. "Redeeming History: Toni Morrison's *Beloved.*" *Female Subjects in Black and White.* Ed. Elizabeth Abel, Barbara Christian, and Helene Moglen. Berkeley and Los Angeles: University of California Press, 1997. 201–20.

Morrison, Toni. *Beloved.* New York: Knopf, 1987.

Nagy, Phyllis. *The Scarlet Letter.* New York: Samuel French, 1995.

"One Minute Interview." Interview with Adina Porter. *Village Voice,* May 14, 1996, 81.

Pearce, Michele. "Alien Nation: An Interview with the Playwright." *American Theatre* 26 (March 1994): 26.

Pochoda, Elizabeth. "'I See Thuh Black Card. . . .'" *The Nation,* May 27, 2002, 36–37.

"Queen Hatshepsut." *King Tut One.* www.kingtutone.com/queens/hatshepsut (visited January 16, 2006).

Rasbury, Angeli. "Pulitzer Winner Parks Talks about Being a First." National Organization for Women, Women's E-News. www.now.org/eNews/april2002/041102parks.html (visited January 1, 2008).

Rayner, Alice, and Harry J. Elam, Jr. "Unfinished Business: Reconfiguring History in Suzan-Lori Parks's *The Death of the Last Black Man in the Whole Entire World.*" *Theatre Journal* 46.4 (December 1994): 447–61.

"Remarks on Parks 1." Hunter College Symposium on Suzan-Lori Parks: Critics and Scholars. www.hotreview.org/articles/remarksparks1.htm (visited January 19, 2006).

"Remarks on Parks 2." Hunter College Symposium on Suzan-Lori Parks: Directors. www.hotreview.org/articles/Remarksparks2.htm (visited January 19, 2006).

"River Jordan." www.holysites.com/riverjordan.htm (visited January 16, 2006).

Robertson, Campbell. "Public Theater's Play a Day Goes National." *New York Times,* June 21, 2006, B2.

Robertson, Campbell. "What Do You Get If You Write a Play a Day? A Lot of Premieres." *New York Times,* November 30, 2006, B3.

Robinson, Marc. *The Other American Drama*. Cambridge: Cambridge University Press, 1994.

Ryan, Katy. "'No Less Human': Making History in Suzan-Lori Parks's *The America Play*." *Journal of Dramatic Theory and Criticism* 13 (Spring 1999): 81–94.

Schiebinger, Londa. *Nature's Body: Gender in the Making of Modern Science*. Cambridge: Harvard University Press, 1989.

Shange, Ntozake. *for colored girls who have considered suicide/when the rainbow is enuf*. 1977. New York: Collier Macmillan, 1989.

Shange, Ntozake. *See No Evil: Prefaces, Essays & Accounts, 1976–1983*. San Francisco: Momo, 1984.

Shepard, Sam. *True West*. Garden City, NY: Doubleday, 1982.

Shewey, Don. "An Eccentric Ringmaster Creates His Own Circus." *New York Times*, April 14, 1996, Arts and Leisure, 5, 34.

Solomon, Alisa. "Signifying on the Signifyin': The Plays of Suzan-Lori Parks." *Theater* 21.3 (1990): 73–80.

Sova, Kathy. "A Better Mirror: An Interview with the Playwright." *American Theatre* 17.3 (March 2000): 32.

Stein, Gertrude. *The Making of Americans*. Normal, IL: Dalkey Archive, 1995.

Stein, Gertrude. *A Stein Reader*. Ed. Ulla E. Dydo. Evanston, IL: Northwestern University Press, 1993.

"Suzan-Lori Parks." Lit Links—Drama. http://www.bedfordstmartins.com/litlinks/drama/parks.htm (visited January 1, 2008).

Thornton, Brian. *101 Things You Didn't Know about Lincoln*. Avon, MA: Adams Media, 2006.

365NYC: First Sundays Series. Program published by the Public Theater, March 2007.

Vorlicky, Robert. "Blood Relations: Kennedy and Kushner." *Tony Kushner: New Essays on the Art and Politics of the Plays*. Ed. James Fisher. Jefferson, NC: McFarland, 2006. 41–55.

Walat, Kathryn. "These Are the Days." *American Theater* 23.9 (November 2006): 26–31, 81–83.

Wallace, Michele. "The Hottentot Venus." *Village Voice*, May 21, 1996, 31.

Wilmer, S. E. "Restaging the Nation: The Work of Suzan-Lori Parks." *Modern Drama* 43 (Fall 2000): 442–52.

Wilson, August. *Two Trains Running*. New York: Dutton/Penguin, 1992.

Wilson, Harriet E. *Our Nig, or, Sketches from the Life of a Free Black*. New York: Vintage, 1983.

"Women of Color Women of Words." www.scils.rutgers.edu/~cybers/imp.html (visited January 1, 2008).

Worthen, W. B. "Citing History: Textuality and Performativity in the Plays of Suzan-Lori Parks." *Essays in Theatre/Etudes Théâtrales* 18.1 (November 1999): 3–22.

Wright, Richard. *Native Son.* 1940. New York: Harper Perennial, 1998.

Yaffe, David. "Sex and the City." *The Nation,* December 27, 1999, 32–34.

Young, Jean. "The Re-objectification and Re-commodification of Saartjie Baartman in Suzan-Lori Parks's *Venus.*" *African American Review* 31 (1997): 699–708.